HOME DECOR IDEA BOOK
SLIPCOVERS

HOME DECOR IDEA BOOK
SLIPCOVERS

JACKIE VON TOBEL

GIBBS SMITH
TO ENRICH AND INSPIRE HUMANKIND

First Edition
17 16 15 14 13   5 4 3 2 1

Text and illustrations © 2013 Jackie Von Tobel

Published by
Gibbs Smith
P.O. Box 667
Layton, Utah 84041

1.800.835.4993 orders
www.gibbs-smith.com

Designed by Michelle Thompson | Fold and Gather Design
Printed and bound in China
Gibbs Smith books are printed on either recycled, 100% post-consumer waste,
FSC-certified papers or on paper produced from sustainable PEFC-certified
forest/controlled wood source. Learn more at www.pefc.org.

Library of Congress Cataloging-in-Publication Data

Von Tobel, Jackie.
  Home décor idea book slipcovers / Jackie Von Tobel. — First Edition.
    pages cm
  ISBN 978-1-4236-2010-5
1. Slip covers. 2. Interior decoration. I. Title. II. Title:
Slipcovers.
  TT395.V66 2013
  746.9'5—dc23
                              2012037729

For Arnie, JT, Geordie and Angelica

CONTENTS

PREFACE

My dear readers, writing and illustrating books on soft treatment design is a passion that I have been very fortunate to be able to follow over the past few years thanks to my publisher, Gibbs Smith, my marvelous editor, Madge Baird, and their team. This book is intended to provide design inspiration and basic knowledge to the reader. The designs shown within these pages are common, widely used standards within the interior design industry. The illustrations are my interpretation of those designs and of combinations of standard design elements used in the construction of slipcovers.

My goal is to produce a visual reference for soft treatment design that is a standard within the industry for the purpose of improving communication between the designer and the workroom as well as giving the designer a visual jump start as she prepares her original designs. This is a labor of love for me and is a testament to my passion for the industry that I have worked in for over twenty years.

All of the images and illustrations in this book are original and have not been reproduced from any other publication or product. Any resemblance to any other publication or product is coincidental and is derived as a result of the common, standard, and historical elements used to design and construct all slipcovers.

It has been a pleasure writing and illustrating this book and I hope that you find it inspirational and educational. Thank you for the tremendous support and acceptance you have given me over the past few years.

Sincerely,

Jackie Von Tobel

INTRODUCTION

Nothing gives an old piece furniture a new lease on life like a beautiful slipcover. This book will provide you with the inspiration and knowledge necessary for you to make an informed decision about the style, design and construction of the slipcovers you want to sew or have sewn.

While this book does not contain step-by-step instructions on how to construct each design, it does discuss the key points of each cover and its basic design elements. Whether you choose to sew your covers yourself or use a professional workroom service, the information available in this book will assist you along the way.

For countless years, slipcovers were viewed primarily as a utilitarian product meant to provide a temporary fix for an old piece of furniture or a dust cover to prevent wear and tear. Remember your grandmother's clear vinyl chair covers? Today's slipcovers are an integral part of the design in modern interiors. They still serve a purpose but also provide flexibility and variety to an interior that traditional furnishings do not. Slipcovers are perhaps the single most impactful tool in the modern design arsenal.

My goal in writing this book is to provide a visual resource for design ideas. Many of the covers you will see in this book can be made at home by sewers who have a moderate to intermediate sewing capability. Others require the skilled expertise of a seasoned slipcover professional.

Home Design Idea Book: Slipcovers is an indispensable tool written to help you navigate the process of design. It contains hundreds of illustrations of creative ideas and common slipcover styles that can be made as shown or can inspire you to create unique designs of your own.

The information and techniques outlined in the first chapter will walk you through the many steps of slipcover design and construction:

Selecting Furniture
Not every piece of furniture is suitable for slip covering. Use the guidelines and checklist in the first chapter to determine if your furniture passes the test.

Selecting Fabric
Fabric selection is extremely important to produce a well-fitting and long-lasting slipcover. Follow the recommendations in this section to avoid costly mistakes.

Measuring Accurately
Fitting a slipcover is like tailoring a fine suit; the measurements must be precise and accurate. Learn simple ways to ensure a perfect fit.

Choosing an Appropriate Design
Use the basic design fundamentals and guidelines outlined here to choose the appropriate design for your specific piece of furniture.

Adding Embellishments
Small touches such as welting or trim can make a huge impact in your slipcover design. Choose from the individual embellishments in this book to personalize your design.

* * *

Whether you decide to sew your own or choose to rely on a professional to make your slipcovers, I hope you enjoy the process of choosing the right design for your piece of furniture.

SLIPCOVER BASICS

A BIT OF HISTORY

The slipcover has a long and historic past beginning in medieval times where furniture was scarce and usually consisted of a hard stool or bench. Seat cushions made of rough fabrics were filled with straw and used to soften the hard seats of the well to do.

Slipcovers continued to be a luxury confined to the wealthy during the renaissance when furniture began to be upholstered in rich silk brocades and other pricy textiles. Plain slipcovers were used most of the time to protect this expensive fabric from wear and tear. They were removed only on special occasions when the owner chose to show off his finery to friends and guests.

During the seventeenth century furniture had become more readily available to the wealthy as well as other household luxuries and embellishments. The size of the homes of the rich had also increased substantially with many rooms used only on special occasions. This led to the creation of the dust cover; a loosely fitted white cover made from muslin or linen that covered all articles of value within a room when it was not in use. Furnishings at that time were true works of art and extremely expensive, they were meant to last for generations. The dust cover was a way for the owner to protect his valuables from the sun, insects, humidity, mold and mildew and other forms of wear and tear that would devalue his investments. Dust covers were made for chandeliers, wall sconces, mirrors, and anything else that could be covered.

As the eighteenth century began, more people had the means to acquire large homes and fine furnishings. In England it became popular to cover the heavy upholstery common in the day with bright cotton or linen tailored slipcovers for the summer season. These soft, lightweight fabrics were more comfortable on the skin in the warmer months and they served the practical purpose of absorbing moisture and protecting the expensive upholstery beneath. As time went by, the slipcover became an integral part of the design scheme, being constructed in fabrics that matched or coordinated with the interiors in which they were placed. This trend moved across the English channel to France where it was adopted enthusiastically by the design community, spawning a new industry of slipcover artisans to fill the demand.

During the Victorian era, immigrants coming to America from Europe brought with them the trade of slipcover tailoring. Fine furnishings at that time in America were still somewhat hard to come by and much of it was imported at great expense from Europe. Therefore, slipcovers were a key tool in preserving fine furnishings. It became commonplace for the entire household to be outfitted with bright printed slipcovers for the warm season, which were then packed away for the winter.

As the industrial revolution took hold across the globe, furniture became made on the production line. Pieces were no longer made bespoke by artists who had trained for years at their craft. The cost of wood and other materials dropped due to advances in milling and transportation. More and more furniture was made within traveling distance of the customer. These and many other factors made furniture more affordable and accessible to the masses. At the same time the grand estates of the wealthy were diminishing as was the demand for artisanal furnishings. With the lower cost of furnishings in place, individual pieces of furniture became less important to the owner. Therefore, the priority of protecting them with slipcovers became less important although their appeal as a decorative tool has remained strong.

In recent years there has been a strong resurgence in the popularity of slipcovers. Individuals are taking notice of the throw-away tendencies of our society and are opting to repurpose and reuse their furnishings. Slipcovers are a great way to revamp an old piece and add new life to an interior or exterior space. We have also become accustom to a great variety in our surroundings and the cycle of trends seems to move at an ever increasing pace. Slipcovers allow us to adopt trends in color and style easily without having to purchase new furnishings.

THE BENEFITS OF USING SLIPCOVERS

Slipcovers have remained popular for centuries because they can quickly add style, color and pattern to a room while providing important functions as well.

Fashion

Slipcovers can quickly bring new life to old or outdated furnishings.

A slipcover will allow you to utilize existing furnishings in a new décor scheme.

They allow you to significantly alter the look of a room instantly whether as a permanent change or as a seasonal variation.

Slipcovers can allow you to have a variety of looks for one room that you can change frequently, seasonally or on a whim.

Function

A slipcover can protect expensive upholstery fabrics and delicate wood frames and finishes from daily wear and tear.

They can hide flaws in furnishings or cover items that would not fit into the design scheme, allowing them to blend in.

Slipcovers can be made to be washed regularly so they are a great solution for furniture in high-use areas or pieces that will be used with kids and pets.

Adding a fabric cover can soften hard-frame furnishings and add more comfort. They can be fitted with padding for extra comfort in specific areas such as the seat and the back.

Economy

As a slipcover hides most or all of a piece it is covering, using thrift store finds, hand-me-downs, and unmatched pieces is a viable and economic option.

When comparing the cost of refinishing or reupholstering your furniture versus slipcover construction, covers are considerably less expensive.

Fabrics such as cotton duck and union cloth that are typically used for slipcovers are less expensive than those used as permanent upholstery.

FURNITURE SELECTION

Not every piece of furniture is a great candidate for a slipcover. There are several key factors that you must consider when evaluating your furnishings before you cover them. Go through the checklist below to see if your piece is up to the task.

How Suitable Is Your Furniture's Profile?

In general, the more curves, rounded edges, or fancy shaping on your piece of furniture, the more difficult the fitting of your slipcover will be. If you plan to tackle the construction of your cover yourself, it is best to choose pieces that have the following qualities:

Strong, straight lines
Gradual, gentle curves
Right angles
Good proportion and scale

You may want to leave the more difficult jobs for the professionals.

Does Your Furniture Have Good Bones?

All furniture, whether exposed frame or fully uphol-stered, has an inner structure that gives it its shape and provides structure and strength. It is important to give the frame a thorough review to see if it is in less than prime condition. You don't want to go to the expense of covering a piece that is in bad shape. Look for the following red alerts:

Loose or Broken Joints

If your piece has a hardwood frame that is in good shape but has loosened over time and become creaky or wobbly, it may still be worth the cost of having the frame repaired. If the wobbly piece has a cheaply made frame put together using particle board and staples in its construction, you may want to find a different one.

Old Repairs

Has your piece been doctored before? Look for glue, nails, or staples. Does the repair look stable or is it a temporary fix that will not stand the test of time?

Dry Rot

Dry rot is the term used for decay to the wooden structure of your furnishings caused by a wood fungus. It cannot be repaired. The affected area has to be replaced.

Insect Damage

Look for worm holes or signs of burrowing by termites. Excess wood dust at the joints can be a clue. If you suspect insects but are not sure, use the tip of a knife and press it into the wood. If it goes in easily, you may have a problem.

Foot Wear

Check the wear and tear on the feet of the piece to determine if they are level. Over time legs and feet can wear unevenly, causing the piece of furniture to wobble or lean. Place the piece on a flat, hard surface and do a visual inspection of the feet to be sure they are all firmly planted on the floor. Look for obvious cracks and splits that might cause a problem in the future.

Lead Paint

Many antique pieces that can be found in flea markets or antiques shops have been painted, sometimes with many layers of paint over the years. It is important to check for lead paint on your piece, especially if you have children or pets. Try a product called Lead Check at http://leadcheck.com.

Is the Upholstery Ready for a Cover?

Even though you are going to cover your piece of furniture, you want to be sure that the upholstery on the piece is in good shape and isn't holding any unwanted surprises. Inspect your piece thoroughly for the following:

Tears and Tatters

It is important that the fabric under your slipcover be sturdy and able to maintain the shape of the padding inside in order to support the cover. If there are obvious tears, holes, or tatters in the fabric, they will show through the slipcover. Cloth tape or fabric patches applied with iron-on binding webbing can be a quick solution to minor problems.

Slippery or Rough Fabric

If your furniture is upholstered in leather or vinyl, be prepared for your slipcover to slide around more than you would probably like. At the other end of the spectrum, if your fabric is very rough, as with terry cloth or heavy chenille, your covers may bunch up and twist with wear. The best fabric surfaces for slipcovers are tightly woven, smooth or lightly textured weaves.

Bad Padding

Take a look at all areas of upholstery on your piece, including loose cushions. Is the padding still fluffy and shaped appropriately for the piece? If it is lumpy, compressed, misshapen, or deteriorating due to age, this might be a sign to find a new item to cover. Many times the upholstered area on the frame are fine, but there may be a problem with the loose cushions. These are easily replaced to give your furniture a new lease on life. See the resource guide for details.

Shot Springs

Many chairs and sofas will have spring construction that supports the seat. Remove the loose cushions if there are any and sit on the piece. Listen for creaking or scraping sounds. Look for wires or springs poking through the upholstery. Check to be sure there is no sagging or slanting in the seat.

Destroyed Decking

Underneath your seat cushions, there is most likely a muslin decking that covers the springs and inner support system of your furniture. Check to be sure that it is not ripped or frayed. Also, check the underside of the chair to see if the exposed webbing or muslin is in good shape.

Sun Rot

UV Rays can destroy upholstery fabric in short order, leaving it thin, frayed and unstable. Check for extreme fading, powdering and hardening of the fabric to avoid continuing problems.

Mold and Mildew

Water can be one of the most destructive elements to fine furnishings and sometimes one of the hardest to detect. Give your piece a visual check for water stains or spotty black discoloration from mold and mildew. Don't forget the smell test!

Pet Damage

An untrained pet can wreak havoc on a nice piece of furniture. Check for obvious signs of chewing on the wood and then the dreaded stains and smells of pet urine. The most likely areas affected will be the legs and seat. Again, be sure to smell the chair.

Bed Bugs

In recent years the bed bug has made a huge resurgence in the United States and upholstered furnishings make a fine home for these pesky pests. Look in seams and along welting for the small black dots that are a sure sign of an infestation.

CHOOSING THE RIGHT STYLE COVER

Slipcovers are like couture fashions for your furniture; they come in all shapes, sizes and designs.

A slipcover that is appropriate for a wood frame dining chair may not be appropriate for a fully upholstered occasional chair or a sofa. Here are a few of the different types of covers and the pieces of furniture for which they are most appropriate.

Chairs, Barstools, Settees and Benches

Seat covers: Loose-fitting or tailored slips that cover the seat area of your furniture

Seat cushions: Tailored covers that include a padded cushion for the seat area

Back covers: Loose-fitting or tailored slips that cover the back of your piece of furniture

Back cushions: Fitted covers that include a padded area on the inside back of the chair for added comfort

Fitted one-piece covers: Tailored slipcovers that cover most of a piece of furniture and are constructed in one piece

Loose one-piece covers: Loosely tailored slipcovers that cover most of a piece of furniture and are constructed in one piece

Occasional Chairs, Chaise Lounges, Sofas and Upholstered Benches

Fitted one-piece covers: Tailored slipcovers that cover most of a piece of furniture and are constructed in one piece

Loose one-piece covers: Loosely tailored slipcovers that cover most of a piece of furniture and are constructed in one piece

Headboards

Fitted one-piece covers: Tailored slipcovers that cover most of the headboard and are constructed in one piece

CHOOSING THE APPROPRIATE COVER

Furniture with a fully exposed frame and a hard or upholstered seat is not usually well suited for a full slipcover. The cover needs some soft surfaces to cling to in order to maintain its shape and position on the furniture, and this type of frame does not offer that. It is, however, a great candidate for seat and back cushions and covers.

A piece of furniture with an exposed wood frame, having the added softness of an upholstered back, can be covered with a full slipcover or a one- or two-piece chair cover. It can also be covered with a two-piece cover, if you desire.

Although this chair has a wood-framed back and arms, it is still a good candidate for a full cover because of its large areas of upholstery.

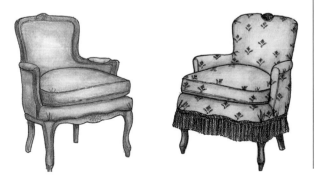

MAKING YOUR FABRIC SELECTION

Choosing an appropriate fabric for your slipcover design is essential to ensure that it looks great and wears well and long. All fabrics are not suitable and some work better for slipcovers than others depending on the design and the intended use. The first step in making your selection is to ask yourself or your client a few basic questions.

How will your furniture be used? Is it going to be placed in a high-traffic area? Will kids and pets be sitting on it?
Covers used on furniture in high-traffic areas of your home will need to be made of sturdy, stable fabrics that can be cleaned easily. Low-maintenance fabrics such as 100 percent cottons or polyester-cotton blends may help your cover to retain its shape and stay in place. Natural fibers such as linen will wrinkle and need more maintenance than blends. Medium-weight cotton ducks, denims and twill are a great choice for kid-friendly covers.

If you have pets, consider the color of their fur when selecting your fabric. Black pet hair on a beautiful white linen slipcover is not a stylish look.

Will your furniture be placed in direct sunlight or close to heat registers or vents?
Natural fibers are more susceptible to sun rot than synthetic blends. And dark or vivid colors will fade quickly if placed in direct sunlight. If you are placing your furnishings near a window or in a place that gets intense light, you may want to consider a polyester or polyester-cotton blend fabric to combat sun fading and heat shrinkage.

When making slipcovers for outdoor furniture, be sure to use fabrics and trims that are specifically rated for outdoor use such as products by Sunbrella. Today these fabrics come in a wide range of solids and prints that can address all of your design needs.

Outdoor fabrics are also being used inside because of their durability and washability. They may be a good choice if your piece will be used by kids or pets.

Will you want to wash your slipcovers periodically, frequently, or not at all?

If you intend to wash your covers, prewash a small section of fabric to see how much the fabric will shrink and how much washing will affect the color. Then, prewash all of your yardage before beginning your project. Take note of the amount of shrinkage in both the length and the width of your fabric and adjust your final yardage requirements to make up for it.

Many times during prewashing, the selvedge or finished edges of the fabric will shrink more than the rest of the yardage. If this is the case, you may want to cut off the selvage after washing but before ironing your fabrics so it will lay flat for cutting.

For covers that will be washed frequently, you may want to use solid colors. White is a universal color for slipcovers because of the ability to use bleach when washing it to remove dirt and stains. When choosing fabric for high-use covers that will be washed frequently, it's best to stick to light solids or washed-out prints with an already faded look to them.

In most cases using trim on washable covers is not advised because most trim is not washable and will have to be removed before you throw your covers into the wash. It will have to be applied again afterwards.

Covers that will not be washed are more suitable for rich-colored and patterned fabrics. These fabrics most likely specify that they should be dry cleaned.

What type of fabric is on the piece you will be covering?

Is your furniture covered in a very dark or very bright and vivid pattern? Will the fabric you are choosing for your cover conceal the pattern or will it show through?

Does the fabric on your piece have a rough texture? Will it be visible through your slipcover fabric?

Are you covering leather or vinyl upholstery? Your cover may slip and slide over those fabrics. Choosing a cover fabric that has some grip to it, like a chenille or velvet, will help you avoid that problem.

SUITABLE FABRICS

Medium-weight, tightly woven, upholstery grade fabrics are the best choice for slipcovers. Your slipcover fabric needs to stand up to the same wear and tear as your upholstery. It can be tempting to use lightweight fabrics that are more suited for drapery and bedding, but those fabrics do not have the strength and durability needed for use as slipcovers.

Appropriate fabrics come in various fibers and blends and are most commonly 54 inches wide.

Natural Fiber Fabrics
    Linen
    Cotton Linen Blends
    Cotton Duck
    Cotton Twill
    Cotton Canvas
    Hemp
    Denim
    Natural or Raw Silk
    Corduroy
    Woolens

Synthetic Fiber Fabrics
    Polyester
    Polyester Cotton Blends
    Faux Suede
    Velvets
    Velour
    Chenille
    Suiting

Fabrics to Avoid
    Stretchy fabrics that contain Spandex or Lycra
    Loosely woven fabrics
    Thin lightweight fabrics
    Quilt weight cottons
    Fabric in widths less than 54 inches
    Heavyweight fabrics
    Ruched or puckered fabrics
    Lightweight silks
    Rayon fabrics

WORKING WITH PATTERNED FABRICS

Slipcovers can be made in solid colors or large patterns, stripes, geometrics and other patterns, but it is important to take into consideration the size and shape of your cover before making your fabric selections.

Large pattern repeats not only require expert pattern matching and motif placement but will increase the yardage requirements for your cover.

Stripes must be planned carefully as to their direction on the piece and can also require some tricky pattern matching at the seams.

Plaids are a favorite for traditional slipcovers but they can be difficult to work with because you have to match the pattern both horizontally and vertically along the seam lines.

Medium-size repeats still require some pattern matching but are more manageable and will only increase the yardage requirements slightly.

Small overall prints can be pieced without regard to the repeat and can be treated almost like a solid fabric.

Border Prints where the area of pattern runs only along the selvedge of your otherwise plain or small patterned yardage are great for slipcovers because the patterned border can be detached and used as an accent.

Pattern Direction
When choosing your fabrics, keep in mind that the pattern direction is important when calculating your yardage and planning your pattern placement.

Typical Pattern
The pattern runs vertically along the length of the fabric. This is typical for most drapery and upholstery fabrics.

Railroaded Pattern
The pattern runs horizontally from selvage to selvage. Railroaded patterns are used primarily for upholstery and can make pattern matching a challenge.

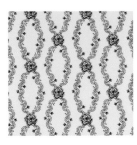

Typical

Railroaded

Railroaded fabrics are usually made specifically for application on upholstery items because of the need for wide width cuts in their construction. If you can find a railroaded pattern you like, your yardage requirement and the amount of cuts required may be reduced.

Pattern Placement
Dominant Primary Pattern

Secondary Pattern

Pattern Dominance
Many fabrics have a motif that includes a primary and secondary pattern. It is important to choose which one you want to highlight when plotting your pattern placement on your piece of furniture.

Pattern Repeats and Pattern Matching

Patterns will always have a vertical and horizontal repeat even if the overall motif is very small. It is important to match these repeats when making your cuts to produce a professional-looking slipcover. Nothing stands out more obviously on a piece of furniture than a misplaced or mismatched repeat. It throws off the balance of the cover and takes away from the overall beauty of the piece that you worked so hard to create. Taking the time to match your patterns perfectly at the beginning of the sewing process will pay off in a great-looking cover at the end.

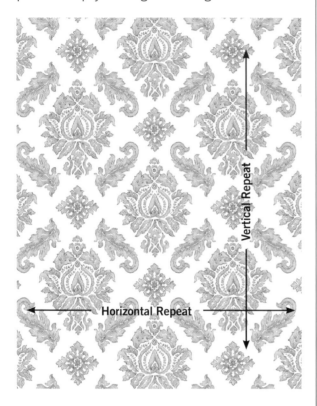

Small Pattern Repeat

Very often a fabric with a small pattern that seems to have little or no repeat will have a larger full-length repeat. This can result in a striping effect when it is used in length. The only way to check for this patterning is to inspect a generous length of the fabric.

Balanced Pattern Match

The pattern that is repeated is a whole motif that is balanced on both selvage edges of the fabric. In this case, the seam runs through the field of the fabric or a secondary pattern when joining cuts and there are no seams running through the primary motif.

Halved Pattern Match

The pattern that is to be repeated is cut in half at each selvage edge of the fabric. In this case the seam will run through the center of the primary motif when joining cuts.

Half Drop Repeat or Drop Match Pattern

The pattern on one selvage edge of a fabric panel will not match straight across to the other edge. The pattern on the right edge of the fabric will be one-half its height up or down from the left edge. Therefore, additional fabric is needed to match the pattern as one-half of the repeat is wasted in making matching cuts.

Straight Repeat or Straight Match Pattern

The pattern is positioned in a straight line across the width of the fabric and is the same on the right side of the fabric as on the left.

Half Drop Pattern Repeat   **Straight Match Pattern Repeat**

Vertical and Horizontal Repeat

This is the distance between the full repeat of a pattern on the face of a fabric going in either a horizontal or vertical direction.

Print-on-Print Repeats

In fabrics such as woven damasks that have a printed pattern on the face, there are two patterns that must be matched; the base pattern of the damask as well as the printed pattern over the top of the base. Failing to match the ground pattern as well as the printed pattern will result in an off-matched ground pattern that will be obvious on the finished cover.

FURNITURE ANATOMY
Dining Chair

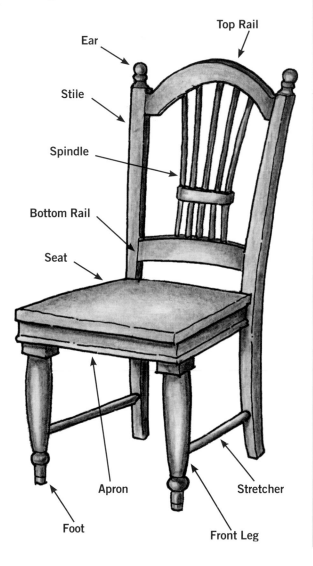

Ear

Top Rail

Stile

Spindle

Bottom Rail

Seat

Apron

Foot

Stretcher

Front Leg

Occasional Chairs and Sofas

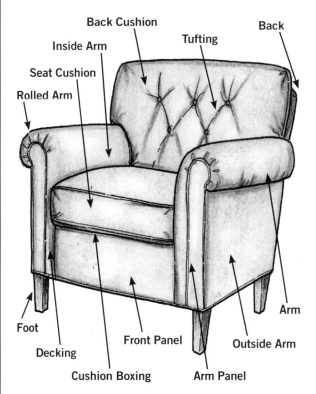

Back Cushion

Inside Arm

Tufting

Back

Seat Cushion

Rolled Arm

Foot

Decking

Front Panel

Cushion Boxing

Arm Panel

Outside Arm

Arm

MEASURING

Accurate measurements are the key to producing a beautiful slipcover, and no matter what style or design you choose, measuring to the nearest fraction of an inch is necessary for a good fit. In order to get these measurements from the curves and angles of a three-dimensional piece of furniture, professional slipcover artisans have developed methods to ensure they get it right every time.

Templates

For certain designs, making a paper or cloth template is the way to go. This method works well on hard surface chairs and chair backs where there is no upholstery to pin the fabric to.

1. Use butcher paper if your surface is flat; muslin or lining cloth if it is curved or angled.

2. Cut a section of paper or fabric larger than the area that you are measuring.

3. Tape your paper or fabric in place using painter's tape or masking tape. If you have trouble getting it to stay in place, use double-stick tape to hold it still.

4. Use tailor's chalk to mark the perimeter of the seat or area you are working on. If you are using paper, you can crease the edge by bending the fabric over the edges to be sure you get all the subtle bends and curves and then mark the fabric or paper with chalk.

5. Remove the fabric or paper and lay flat. Smooth out the contours of the lines you have marked on the paper with a pen or pencil to create a continuous line. You can now add your seam allowances and your ease allowance to your template and then trim it.

Pin-Fitted Muslin Pattern

Most slipcovers require fitting similar to the work done by a seamstress creating a fancy ball gown. Every curve and angle must be taken into account and the fabric must be manipulated to accommodate it. Slipcover artisans use methods similar to dress makers to form fit the cover such as pleating and inserting darts. Just as a seamstress would fit a gown on a dressmaker's form, the slipcover artisan fits the cover right on the piece of furniture. Pins are used to hold the fabric in place and to form the shape to fit the furniture.

This method works well for seat covers, ottomans, benches and small pieces for which you want to make a pattern but that need more fitting than would be possible by making a paper template.

1. Cut a length of inexpensive muslin or lining fabric larger than the area you are fitting and pin it to the flat surface of the area.

2. Assess the curves and angles of the area to see where darts or gathers will be necessary in order to make the fabric fit the profile of the area.

3. Pull the excess fabric into darts, pleats or gathers at the selected points and pin them in place. Place your darts, pleats or gathers in symmetrical order around the area. Do not pin them to the chair as you want the pins to remain in place once you remove the fabric pattern.

4. Using tailor's chalk, mark the perimeter edges of the pattern and mark along the base of any pleats, gathers, or darts. Be sure to mark the fold points of any pleats and all hems and cutouts necessary to complete your pattern, and mark the pleat and dart direction.

5. Trim the excess fabric from the pattern, leaving plenty of room for adjustment.

6. Once you have the area fitted as close as possible and clearly marked, take out the pins that are holding the fabric in place and remove the pattern.

7. Lay out the pattern and remove all the pins. Refine all your lines, including seams, darts, pleats, and gathers, with the tailor's chalk so they are smooth and straight. Using the chalk and a seam allowance guide, mark the cutting edge after adding the seam allowance and ease.

8. Cut out the pattern at the cutting line.

You now have a finished pattern that you can use to make one or multiple cuts.

Reverse Pin Fitting

Most covers have multiple surface areas that need to be accurately fitted, which takes a significant amount of time. Rather than fitting each area individually to create a separate pattern for each and then cutting them out of the finish fabric and piecing the areas together, most slipcover artisans use the reverse pin-fitting method.

The finish fabric is pinned to the furniture face down in the appropriate sections. By applying it face down, the cover is ready to sew once it is pinned together.

The pin-fitting process is preformed on the finish fabric in the same manner as with the muslin pattern. Pleats, gathers, and darts are securely pinned in and then the seams themselves are carefully planned and pinned meticulously in place, allowing for ease of fit. Hems are pinned up and the chair is now essentially covered in reverse.

1. Do a rough trimming of excess fabric.

2. Remove the entire cover, making sure to leave all the fitting and seam pins in place.

3. The cover is now ready to be sewn together.

Reverse Pin Fitting with Welting

Welting is a vital ingredient in producing a professional-looking slipcover. While some styles look fine without it, the majority benefit greatly from its inclusion. Welting is also a stabilizing force for the slipcover, adding strength at the seams of the cover as well as helping the cover to maintain its original shape.

The reverse pin-fitting process can be preformed in the same manner as described in the previous paragraph, with welting, trim or cording inserted between the layers of fabric as the seams are pinned together.

YARDAGE REQUIREMENTS

Every slipcover is unique and needs to be carefully measured before an accurate yardage estimate can be made.

The following chart is a rough estimate for certain standard furniture items to give you an idea of how many yards of fabric your cover may require.

Furniture Type	Without Skirt	With Skirt
Parsons chair	4½	6
Dining arm chair	5	7
Club chair with separate seat cushion	8	12
Club chair with separate seat, back cushion	10	14
Wing back chair, small	5	9
Wing back chair, large	8	12
Slipper chair	7	9
Chaise lounge	7	10
Chaise lounge with removable seat cushion	9	13
Chaise lounge with seat and back cushion	12	16
2-cushion love seat	13	16
4-cushion love seat	14	17
Sofa with 2 cushions (61"–85")	14	19
Sofa with 3 cushions (61"–85")	16	20
Sofa with 4 cushions (61"–85")	17	21
Sofa with 6 cushions (61"–85")	20	24
Sofa with 3 cushions (86"–106")	19	23
Sofa with 6 cushions (86"–106")	23	27
Ottoman up to 24" x 24"	2	4
Ottoman over 24" x 24"	3	5
Round ottoman	6	8

To adjust the amount of yardage needed to accommodate the pattern repeat for your cover, use the following calculations.

3"–14"	15"–19"	20"–27"	28"–38"	37"–45"	46"–54"
10%	15%	20%	25%	30%	35%

SPECIFICATIONS FOR SLIPCOVER CONSTRUCTION

Slipcovers should be constructed to the same high standards as other soft furnishings.

Basic Construction

Heavyweight upholstery thread should be used for all seams and darts for added strength.

All seams should be serged and finished with an overlock stitch unless the tailoring of the cover requires an open seam.

If using an open seam, the selvages should be over-locked for a finished look and to prevent raveling of the fabric, and the seam should be pressed flat.

Curved seams that have been notched or cut to accommodate the angle of the curve should be reinforced with a second row of stitching.

On high-stress areas such as the corners of cushions or arms, a second row or security stitch may be appropriate. In some cases, when using lighter or loosely woven fabrics, twill tape can be used to reinforce corners or stress areas.

Welting or decorative cording with lip should be used on all joined seams if appropriate for the style of your cover.

Lining

Use an iron-on stabilizer or interfacing on light or loosely woven fabrics to add strength and durability.

If the fabric on the piece you are covering has a vivid pattern or color that will show through your cover, you may need to add a layer of lining fabric to your design.

For designs that include full-length skirts or panels, lining may be needed to add stability, volume, and light control.

Trim

For covers that will be washed regularly, trim should be omitted. If you must use trim, it will have to be removed before washing and then be reapplied.

When applying trim to the seat or inner back of your piece, it should be sewn in place.

Other areas that are not in direct contact with the user can be applied using iron-on tape or trim adhesive.

Avoid placing buttons or other bulky embellishments in areas that might create discomfort for the user.

WELTING

Welting is often used in the construction of slipcovers because it serves several different important functions.

Welting adds strength and durability to the seams of your cover.

It adds fine detail to the slipcover and provides a sharp edge to your design.

Welting helps to separate different sections of color or pattern in your design.

Welting provides an interruption in the large areas of the slipcover and can lesson the appearance of a mismatched pattern in the fabric.

COMMON WELT STYLES

Micro Welt

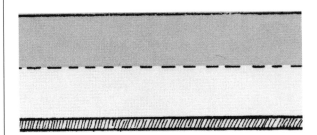

Mini Welt

Standard Welt

(continued)

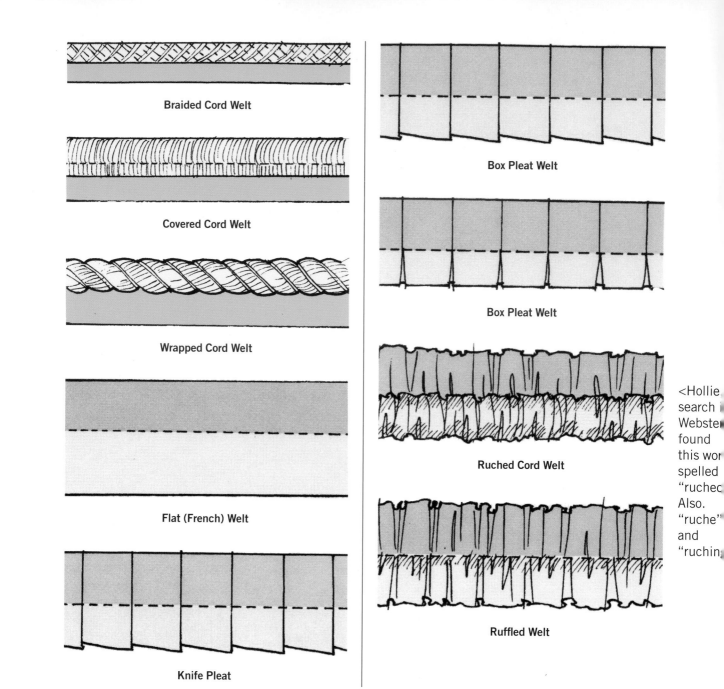

Braided Cord Welt

Covered Cord Welt

Wrapped Cord Welt

Flat (French) Welt

Knife Pleat

Box Pleat Welt

Box Pleat Welt

Ruched Cord Welt

Ruffled Welt

<Hollie
search
Webster
found
this word
spelled
"ruched.
Also,
"ruche"
and
"ruching

PASSEMENTERIE AND DECORATIVE TRIM

Passementerie is the historic French term for the vast category of decorative trims, tassels, and embellishments used to decorate home furnishings.

Decorative trims and embellishments serve as both functional and decorative elements when used on slipcovers.

The main categories are:

Beaded Fringe
Beaded Tapes
Braids Bullion
Cartouches
Cords
Fringes
Galloons
Gimps
Pompons
Ribbons
Rope
Rosettes
Tapes
Tiebacks

Trim can be applied with adhesives, heat bonding tapes, by machine or by hand.

Be aware that most trim can be very delicate and is susceptible to fading and sun rot.

If you want to use trim on a cover that will be placed outdoors or in direct sun, use Sunbrella trims that are specifically manufactured and rated for exterior use.

Most trims are not washable and many are not dry cleanable. If using such trim on a slipcover that will be washed or cleaned, apply the trim in a manner that makes it easily removed for cleaning such as hand tacking or applying it with hook-and-loop tape.

Trim will create additional stiffness to the areas of fabric to which it is applied. Take the size, weight and body of the trim you select into consideration and try to determine what effect it will have on your slipcover.

Trim can often shrink up a bit when taken off the bolt. Always order extra to avoid running short.

Braid

Cord

Grosgrain Ribbon

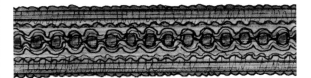

Galloon

Jacquard Looped Fringe

Gimp

Picot Ribbon

Galloon with Scalloped Brush

Moss Fringe

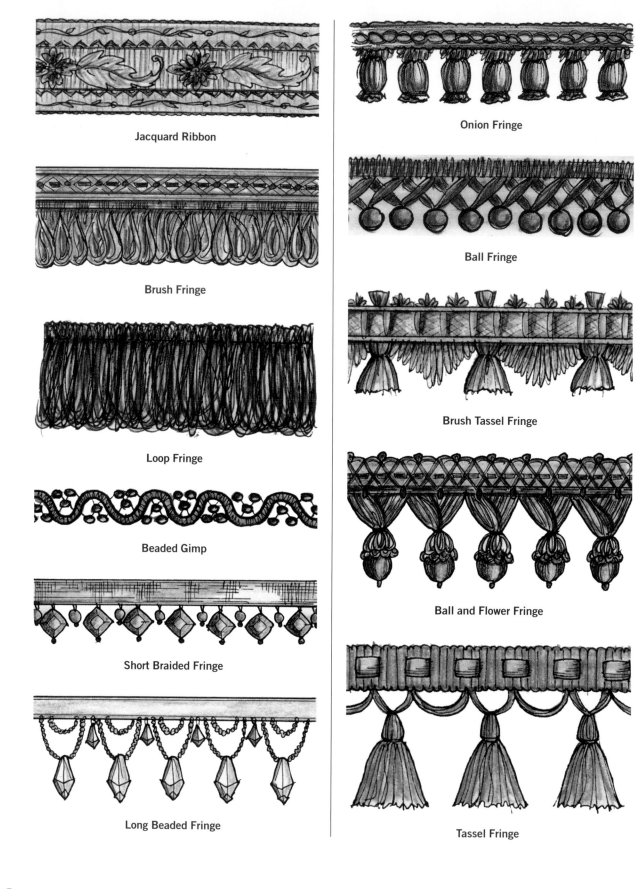

Jacquard Ribbon

Onion Fringe

Brush Fringe

Ball Fringe

Loop Fringe

Brush Tassel Fringe

Beaded Gimp

Ball and Flower Fringe

Short Braided Fringe

Long Beaded Fringe

Tassel Fringe

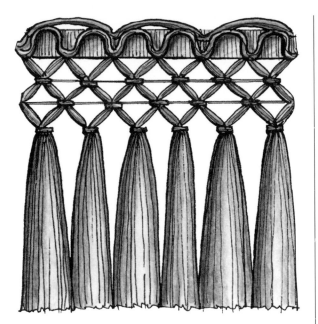

Tied Tassel Fringe

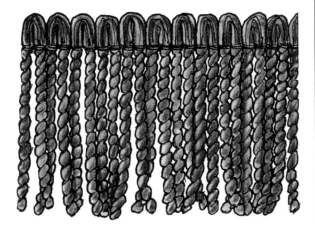

Bullion Fringe

Bell Fringe

Brush and Tassel Fringe

Graduated Tassel Fringe

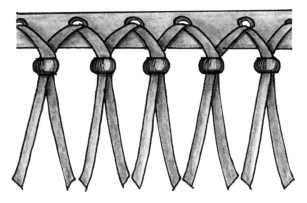

Faux Leather Tied Fringe

SECURING THE SLIPCOVER IN PLACE

Decorative ties or straps are used to secure portions of a cover to the frame of a piece of furniture. Hidden ties or straps are used to add additional security to the cover.

Closures secure the open sections of the cover that are a necessary part of the design in order for the cover to fit over the piece of furniture.

TIES AND STRAPS

To ensure a good fit and to avoid having your cover slide or bunch up when in use, most slipcovers are fitted with ties or other similar devises that secure the cover to the piece of furniture. Some of the most common styles are shown below.

TASSELS

There are many diverse uses for tassels on slipcovers, from pure embellishment to serving as the primary tying mechanism that holds the cover in place on a piece of furniture.

Medallion tassel

Chair Ties

Bullion Tassel

Silk Tassel

Key Tassel

Beaded Chair Ties

CLOSURES

Decorative closures can be a great way to add detail and color to your slipcovers. Here are a few examples:

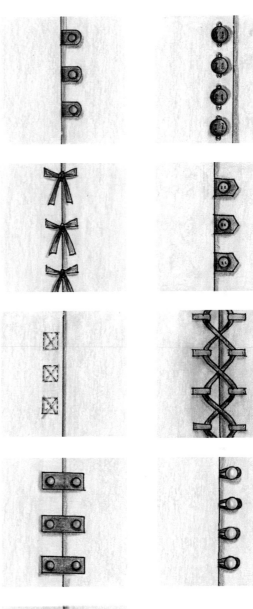

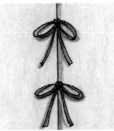

SEAT CUSHIONS

Whether you are adding a new seat cushion to a dining room chair or slip covering a club chair that has loose seat and back cushions, your design may require new seat or back cushion inserts. In order to produce cushions that will look great, last for years, and provide adequate support, it is important to use professional-quality cushion inserts.

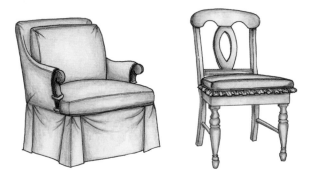

Common Types of Cushion Inserts

There are many different varieties of cushion inserts available today. Thanks to new technologies and man-made fibers and foams, there is a combination for every application.

Most seat and back cushions will require a simple cushion consisting of a foam core with Dacron batting wrapped around it to soften the edges and add loft.

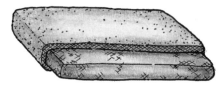

When producing replacements for existing cushions you can make your own using high-density foam wrapped in Dacron batting. You should make a separate cover for the cushion made of lining fabric to keep the batting from shifting inside the finished cover.

Professional-quality replacement cushions are readily available in custom shapes and sizes from many manufacturers. These high-quality inserts can be customized as to content, shape, and style and come covered and ready to install.

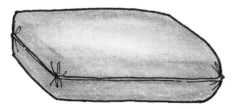

*See the resource guide at the back of the book for replacement cushion suppliers.

Cushion Options

Polyester Fillers

The most widely used cushion inserts are made from a variety of different types of polyester fibers. There are many different brand names, depending on the manufacturer, such as Dacron Holofil. These inserts are machine washable and cost less than most natural fill inserts. New technology has made it possible to manufacture polyester fibers that have a loft and feel somewhat similar to down inserts. Quality and durability vary considerably from manufacturer to manufacturer.

Batting

Batting is a lightweight, lofty, sheet-type cushioning material made of polyester fibers. It is used on seat cushions to wrap the exterior of the more substantial central core of padding used in a cushion in order to add loft and soften hard edges.

Foam

Seating foam comes in a large variety of thicknesses, density, and firmness that allows you to customize the comfort level of your seating.

Water-Resistant Foam

This type of foam is designed for outdoor use. It is formulated to repel water, dry quickly and resist mildew. Be sure to use this type of foam if you are producing outdoor cushions.

Natural Fillers
Premium White Goose Down
Duck Down
Feather / Down Combinations

Down

The term *down* refers to the small fibrous clusters that grow under the feathers in geese and ducks. These fibers posses unique characteristics and an appearance that resembles a mature dandelion cluster. This makes them a perfect fiber for pillow fill. Down has a superior loft that allows it to retain its shape and trap air between clusters, which provides insulation. It releases excess moisture that can build up in the pillow, allowing the pillow to "breathe." Down is cool in the summer and warm in the winter. It is considered to be a superior filling agent in pillows as well as comforters and furnishings.

Goose Down

The down clusters harvested from geese are larger and posses more loft than any other bird. This makes them a superior choice for down fill. Within this category, there are standards that grade the down as superior.

Large clusters

Lightness of pigment with white being the best

Fill power—This term is used to denote the quality of the down. The larger and stronger the cluster, the more fill power it possesses.

Hungarian Goose Down

This has the finest quality of down clusters; they are larger than the norm and are pure white in color.

Duck Down

The clusters of down harvested from ducks are smaller and more coarse than those of geese. Most duck down is collected from ducks raised for food, so they are slaughtered at a young age and the down is not grown to full maturity. Duck down is considered a low-quality down and is sometimes mixed with goose down. Eiderdown is considered to be the ultimate in duck down. It is from a particular species of duck that produces the largest down clusters.

Feather Down Combinations

For most applications, using 100 percent down fill is not appropriate. Down compacts with use and does not hold the shape of the pillow without constant fluffing. Most pillow forms are filled with a combination of down and feathers. The presence of feathers in the mix adds weight and stability to the pillow form.

Within the industry there are several standard mixes available.

Percent of Feathers	Percent of Down
0	100
50	50
25	75
90	10

When choosing the mix for pillow forms, the higher the percentage of feathers to the percentage of down, the heavier and less fluffy they will be.

Feather and down pillow forms must be covered with tightly woven pillow ticking that prevents the down from "leaking" out of the seams. Feather quills can also poke through the ticking and can be an uncomfortable intrusion to the outside of the pillow. Be sure that the forms you are purchasing have leak-proof ticking to prevent these problems.

SEAT AND BACK
CUSHIONS AND COVERS

SEATS

Seat cushions and seat covers are one of the quickest ways to make over your existing furnishings while adding a new level of comfort at the same time.

Seat cushions are most commonly used on furniture with a hard seat. The cover incorporates an interior pad at the seat, which adds comfort and a higher profile to the chair.

Seat covers are used on furniture that already has a padded seat. The cover lays over the existing padded seat and is attached to the chair with ties.

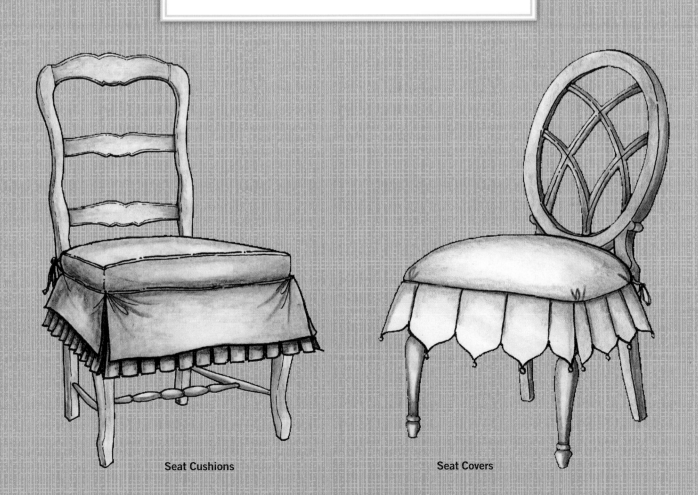

Seat Cushions   **Seat Covers**

Seat: This simple boxed cushion is made more interesting by the addition of a box-pleated band. The pleats are all the same size and run in one direction around the sides of the cushion. Welting is inserted between the top and bottom of the cushion and sides to emphasize the pleated detail.

Seat: The banding on this boxed cushion is shirred a few inches from each corner into the side of the panel, giving emphasis to the four corners of the cushion. Welting is added between the top and bottom and sides to hide any imperfections in the shirring and to separate the three areas.

Seat: Small box pleats are added to the banding of this boxed cushion only at the two front corners. The rest of the banding remains flat. The top and the bottom of the cushion and the pleated banding are separated by welting.

Seat: The side band of this cushion is shirred along the entire perimeter. Welting separates the top and bottom of the cushion from the shirred side banding.

Seat: Ruffled skirts can be a fun addition to any chair cushion and are relatively easy to construct. This example is embellished with a shirred, double-edged ruffle along the hemline of the skirt to add to the feminine design of this cover.

Seat: If fabric bulk is an issue in your design, the under-skirt can be constructed with a flat section at the top and a separate ruffle joined to it just above the hemline. A short ruffle at the intersection of the cover and the skirt draws the eye to the seat and back of the chair and away from the skirt.

Seat: Additional fullness is added to the four legs of this chair cover by tightening the gathers at each corner and cinching in those sections at the seam. The shape at the hem is created by cutting four large scallops into the hem at each side.

Seat: The flat, pointed overskirt of this seat cushion is tailored to fit using darts and gathers at each corner of the seat. The gathered underskirt is added for fullness and length. It also helps the pointed overskirt retain its shape.

Seat: The short skirt on this round seat cover is made by cutting circles on the bias. This allows you to achieve a flat flouncy ruffle rather than a full gathered one. Using a fabric with good drape ability is key to the success of this design.

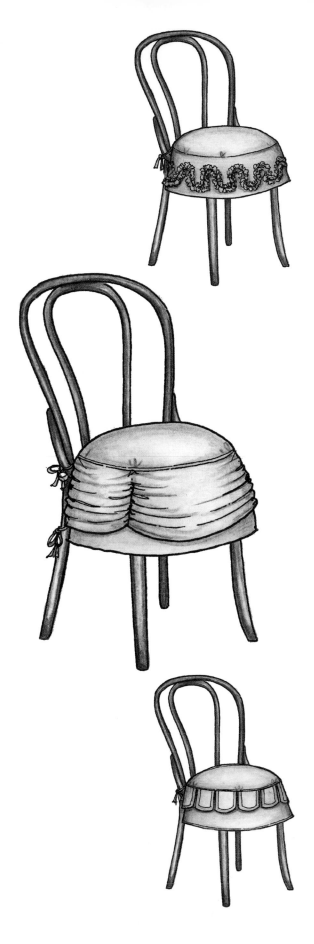

Seat: The flared skirt of this chair cushion is finished off with a sinuous double-sided shirred ruffle. Done in a contracting fabric and attached directly to the face of the skirt, the ruffle reinforces the round lines of the chair back.

Seat: Shirring tape is used on the overskirt of this chair cover to pull up the fabric in accordion swags at each leg of the chair. The flat underskirt is done in a contrasting fabric. The overskirt should be hand tacked to the underskirt to prevent it from riding up.

Seat: Individual sections of fabric follow the perimeter of the round seat to create a uniquely shaped overskirt on this design. Each section is scalloped at the bottom hem and contrasting banding outlines the three exposed edges.

Seat: Decorative banding using a contrasting fabric or trim can be a great way to integrate design elements from your furnishings into your slipcovers. The design from the elaborate back slat of this chair is repeated in a simplified version on the hem of the flat skirt of this boxed cushion.

Seat: The shape, size, and detail of the banding design you choose can assist you in manipulating the finished look of the furniture you are covering. A loose and playful motif will make your chair appear less formal as with this loop design.

Seat: In this design the formal banding motif is centered on each panel rather than running the entire circumference of the skirt. This works well if you are using a thick fabric that would not work well with the increased bulk of the banding at the pleated corners.

Seat: When planning the layout of your banding, be sure to create a motif that can shrink or stretch to fill both the front and back panels as well as the sides. Your motif will have to be sized down in width to fit on the side panels, so you want to select a design that still looks similar to the original once you have adjusted it.

Seat: Leather cording, ribbon or contrasting fabric ties could be used to lace up these corners that are fitted with small grommets on either side of the pleat.

Seat: The same cushion design shown above is fitted with key tassels in this rendering. The tassel cord is threaded through the grommets and the tassels are tied in a knot at each corner.

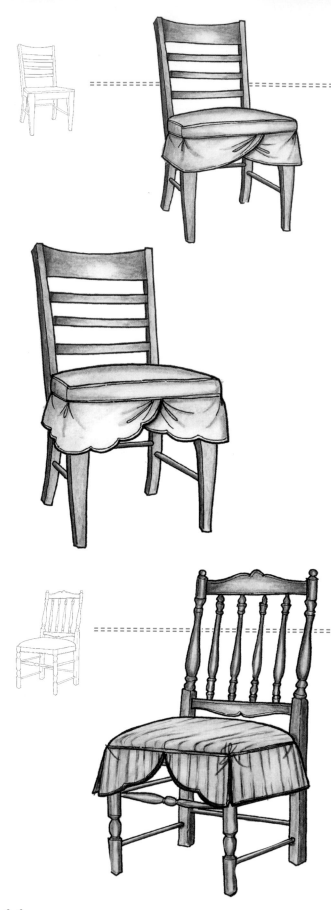

Seat: In this design, two curved panels overlap at the front of the cushion. Volume is created by adding one or two swag pleats at the top of the overlapping edge of the skirt. Tuck pleats are also taken in at each corner of the skirt for additional volume. The result is a pleasantly slouchy skirt that looks great on simple or more detailed furnishings.

Seat: The addition of a scalloped hem to the design above creates a playful look. Be sure to adjust the size of the scallops on the hem so they fall in the right place on the finished skirt. The long point of the scallop at each corner is the starting point for planning the size and length of the scallops.

Seat: These slipcovers are designed with contrasting bias trim wrapping over the edge of the skirt. This edging emphasizes the cut of the skirt while adding some extra strength at the edge.

Seat: An underskirt can be added to any of these covers. Here, a pleated skirt is added. It has additional volume at the four corners of the seat and at the center of the face of the chair.

Seat: There are times when a separate cover for the chair can be topped with an independent seat cushion. In this design the full-length skirt is draped from a decking piece that covers the seat. The boxed cushion is separate and is set on top of the skirt decking.

Seat: Delicate appliqué work follows the curves of the overskirt of this chair cover. The appliqué comes to two peaks at the corners of the front scallop and continues to form fleur-de-lis at each apex. The flat underskirt serves as a backdrop for the appliquéd shapes.

BACKS

M any chairs and other pieces of furniture can benefit from adding a back cushion or cover to their slipcover designs. Back covers and cushions slip over the back of the chair or are tied onto the frame of the chair to provide added comfort and style to it. They also protect the chair frame from wear and tear.

Back cushions incorporate padding into their design, and back covers are unpadded. Both can vary in length, covering all or just part of the chair back. The following chapter shows many of the designs featured in the previous chapter on seat covers and seat cushions with the addition of matching back covers or cushions.

Seat: A flat center pleat marks the middle of the front panel of the skirt of this boxed cushion while crisp knife pleats fold in opposite directions around the sides of the chair.

Back: Back cushions can cover all or part of the chair back depending on the design you choose. This partial padded cover is hung over the top rail of the chair and buttoned in place at the back. Additional straps hold it in place at the bottom rail.

Seat: The flat center pleat of this boxed chair cushion skirt is much larger than the knife pleats at either side of it, which fold outward toward the sides of the chair.

Back: This type of cover, sometimes referred to as a pillow-case cover, is pulled over the chair back. This style works with a chair profile that is straight and has no hard curves or angles that need to be closely fitted. Knife pleats angle outward at the bottom to match the seat cushion design.

Seat: The three pleats in the center of the front of the chair are placed in opposite directions and the remaining pleats follow that direction around the perimeter of the boxed cushion. The front center pleats are repeated on the back center of the skirt.

Back: In this design the back cover is trimmed with a series of knife pleats leading in opposite directions that match the skirt of the chair cushion. The length of the back cover should be adjusted to relate to details in the chair, such as the location of the back slats and spindles.

Seat: This simple flat skirt is embellished with a border of small uniform knife pleats emanating from one central flat pleat at the front of the skirt.

Back: A short back cover gives a more casual look to this design. The length of the cover comes to the bottom of the middle rail of the chair, leaving the bottom rail exposed.

Seat: This simple design uses a small ruffle to decorate the bottom edge of the boxed cushion. Welting is placed between the top and bottom of the cushion and the side banding.

Back: A full back cover can be overpowering when used with a simple seat cushion. Here, the cushion is joined by this small shoulder cover with matching ruffled edging.

Seat: This boxed cushion has a long ruffled skirt at the bottom edge.

Back: Two-piece chair covers can appear to be one piece as with this design. The simplicity of the back cover works well with the flouncy chair cover design. Large bows at each side appear to tie the two pieces together but are actually meant to secure the back cover to the chair stiles.

Seat: Multiple ruffles and a shirred side banding add texture and volume to this boxed chair cushion.

Back: Ruched fabric banding is placed between the front and back sides of this back cover to match the boxed seat cushion.

Seat: Small ruffles make up the welting on both the seat cushion and back cover of this design. This type of welting is useful when working with fabrics that are difficult to pattern match or when joining two different prints together.

Back: Small ruffles make up the welting on both the seat cushion and back cover of this design. This type of welting is useful when working with fabrics that are difficult to pattern match or when joining two different prints together.

Seat: Inverted pleats are placed at the corner of this chair cushion skirt to create volume at the four legs of the chair.

Back: The decorative finials or "ears" on the side rails of this chair are a fun part of the chair design that you may not want to cover. They are also a difficult shape and would no doubt ruin the lines of any full cover. In these designs the ears are intentionally exposed and shown off.

Seat: On this cushion, shirring is added to the center sections of the cushion skirt with each corner pinching in to create volume at each leg of the chair.

Back: The long ruffle of this seat cushion is given balance by the two shorter ruffles at the bottom of the back cover. To reduce bulk, avoid stacking the two ruffled layers on top of one another. Apply the top ruffle and then insert a short extension of the cover base and then apply the bottom ruffle directly to it.

Seat: The hem of this boxed cushion skirt is embellished with a zigzag banding done in a contrasting fabric.

Back: Zigzag appliquéd hems look great on this matching chair cushion and back cover. Adding elements that have a sense of humor and playfulness to your designs can really jazz up a space.

Seat: A scalloped border follows the edge of the skirt on this boxed cushion.

Back: Adding a layer of iron-on quilt batting to the face of your back covers can add a bit of extra comfort to a hard chair. The side panels and back can be left unpadded so there is not much additional bulk at the seams.

Seat: Long box pleats make up the skirt of this boxed cushion. Welting is placed between the top and bottom of the cushion and the side banding.

Back: This small back pad is held in place with multiple ties that go from front to back and over the top and bottom rails to tie the pad in place. It is important to place your tie locations to correspond to specific points on the chair frame that are the best choice for securing your pad tightly.

Seat: Deep box pleats at the four corners of this skirt add interest to its flat profile. Interfacing or stiffener can add much needed body and stability to a flat skirt such as in this design.

Back: This type of back pad is double sided and is the same in the back as in the front. It folds over the top of the chair back and ties around the stiles to hold it in place.

Seat: The number and size of the pleats you use on a skirt can dramatically change the look of the finished product. In this design three equally spaced box pleats form the front of the skirt while the sides and back are flat panels.

Back: Less is more in this cute design, which provides lumbar comfort and leaves the attractive top rail of the chair exposed. The small back cushion is designed to cover the three middle slats of the chair and to follow their contours.

Seat: When trying to achieve a less tailored look, try creating a flat skirt with pleats at each corner using a soft prewashed fabric without using interfacing or stiffener.

Back: This pillowcase-style cover is made up of a box-pleated border that matches the long skirt of the seat cushion. The corners of the bottom of the back cover angle downward at the edges to follow the lines of the bottom chair rail.

Seat: As shown in this design, small box pleats make a great border, banding, or hem detail for slipcovers. They add a wealth of detail without being overly fussy or frilly.

Back: Long fabric ties at each side of this simple back cover cinch in the excess fabric and hold the back cover in place on this chair. The seat cushion has matching ties that are used to secure it in place at each stile.

Seat: To maintain the crisp look of the long pleats in this design, use a natural fiber fabric that can be pressed at high heat to set the pleats. This will ensure that your cover will retain its shape.

Back: A shorter version of the box-pleated seat cushion skirt is used to border the bottom of the tailored back cover of this design. The bottom rail of the chair back is left exposed.

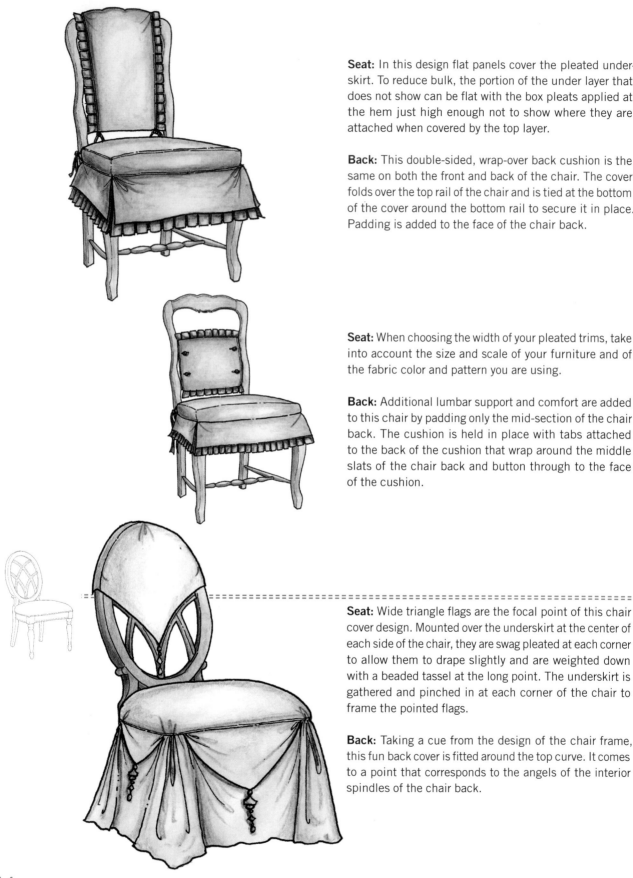

Seat: In this design flat panels cover the pleated under-skirt. To reduce bulk, the portion of the under layer that does not show can be flat with the box pleats applied at the hem just high enough not to show where they are attached when covered by the top layer.

Back: This double-sided, wrap-over back cushion is the same on both the front and back of the chair. The cover folds over the top rail of the chair and is tied at the bottom of the cover around the bottom rail to secure it in place. Padding is added to the face of the chair back.

Seat: When choosing the width of your pleated trims, take into account the size and scale of your furniture and of the fabric color and pattern you are using.

Back: Additional lumbar support and comfort are added to this chair by padding only the mid-section of the chair back. The cushion is held in place with tabs attached to the back of the cushion that wrap around the middle slats of the chair back and button through to the face of the cushion.

Seat: Wide triangle flags are the focal point of this chair cover design. Mounted over the underskirt at the center of each side of the chair, they are swag pleated at each corner to allow them to drape slightly and are weighted down with a beaded tassel at the long point. The underskirt is gathered and pinched in at each corner of the chair to frame the pointed flags.

Back: Taking a cue from the design of the chair frame, this fun back cover is fitted around the top curve. It comes to a point that corresponds to the angels of the interior spindles of the chair back.

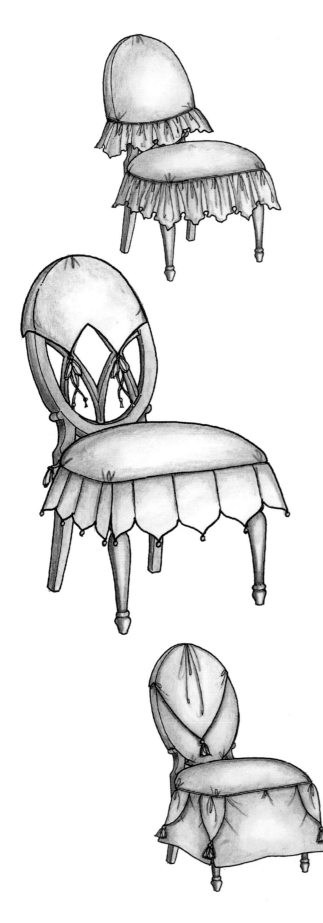

Seat: A zigzag-shaped hem is used on the ruffled skirt of this seat cover to reinforce the pointed shapes seen in the back slats of the chair.

Back: Matching ruffles with a zigzag edge are the common design element in this chair back cover and chair cushion. The ruffle on the chair back is made shorter than the skirt to keep the entire design in proportion to the chair design.

Seat: This seat cover has a skirt constructed by joining individual sections that each come to a point at the hem. When sewn together, they create a zigzag hem that is embellished with beads at each point.

Back: This cover also follows the lines of the chair back. It ends in two points with long ties that secure the back panel to the front through the spindles of the chair back. The ties are embellished with beads at the ends.

Seat: The pointed flags at each corner of this chair cover are tuck pleated at the center to create volume that allows the flags to wrap around the corners without flattening. Key tassels weigh down the points of each flag so they hang properly.

Back: In this highly tailored design, the entire chair back is covered and a second layer of fabric is draped from the top of the back, ending in a point at the bottom that is embellished with a tassel. A pleat is centered at the top for added volume.

Seat: If you prefer a clean look and do not want to use decorative straps or ties to attach your cushion to your chair, use hidden straps that meet at the underside of the chair and attach with hook-and-loop tape.

Back: This simple back cover is trimmed with a flat border that is pleated at its four corners. This border matches the overskirt of the chair cushion.

Seat: The boxed seat cushion of this cover is bordered with a double skirt. The overskirt is topped at each corner with two contrasting squares of fabric that are pinch pleated in the center to add a bit of volume.

Back: A light layer of padding is added to the contrasting, center panel of this chair back cover to give the design a bit more substance and a variety of texture.

Seat: This tailored seat cushion has a flat skirt pleated at the two front corners and split at the back two corners. It is embellished with a double-pointed tab and buttons on the two front corners.

Back: Long contrasting straps that match the detailing on the chair cushion are attached at the back of this short cover. The straps wrap under the cover and around the back rail and then fold over the top to button in place in order to secure the cover to the chair.

Seat: Separate rectangles of contrasting fabric make up the overskirt of this double-layer boxed cushion. The lighter fabric of the under cushion highlights the detail of the design.

Back: This design is reminiscent of vintage, tuck and roll, car seat upholstery with a center panel that has small tucks along its length.

Seat: When planning the number of scallops, be sure that they work when evenly placed at the front and at the side of the chair. Fewer scallops will fit at the side panel.

Back: A center contrasting panel with a scalloped edge at each side is the focal point of this back cover. This panel continues over the top of the chair and down the back.

Seat: In this version of the scalloped skirt the underskirt is flat and pleated at each corner while the top skirt is made up of four separate scalloped edge sections.

Back: The shoulders of this back cover are topped with a second layer of contrasting fabric edged in scallops to match the skirt on the chair cushion.

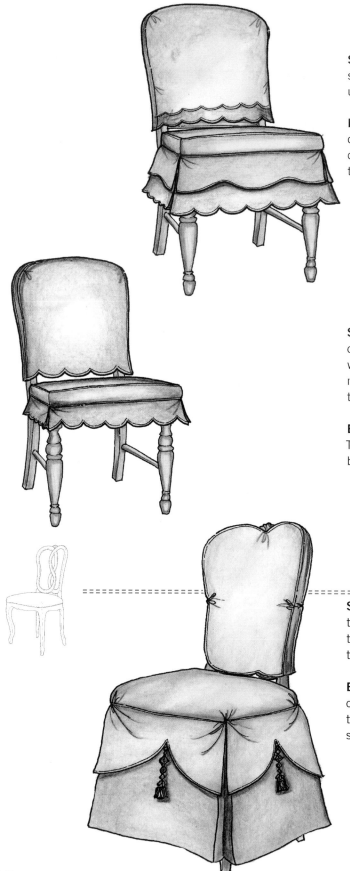

Seat: Adding a sinuous curve to the overskirt of this boxed seat cushion brings it extra attention. The scalloped underskirt acts as a foil to that curve.

Back: In keeping with the double layer design of this chair cushion skirt, the back cover is made with a second layer of contrasting fabric that projects out from underneath the scalloped edge of the top layer.

Seat: A short scalloped skirt is added to this boxed seat cushion. The hem is planned to terminate at each corner with the long point of the scallop at the pleat fold. This makes the scallop appear to fold around the corner of the chair cover.

Back: Simplicity is the key to the success of this design. The scalloped edges of the chair cushion skirt and the back cover tie the two pieces together.

Seat: The tailored skirt of this pretty chair seat cover is topped with an overskirt that curves up from both sides to a peak in the center that is embellished with a beaded tassel.

Back: The matching back cover follows the sinuous curves of the chair frame and is designed with an opening at the top for the carved detail at the center of the back to show through

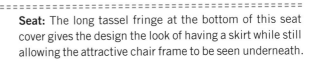

Seat: The long tassel fringe at the bottom of this seat cover gives the design the look of having a skirt while still allowing the attractive chair frame to be seen underneath.

Back: The back cover uses the same decorative tassel fringe to create a border that emphasizes the rolling shape of the shoulders of the chair.

Seat: The skirt of this cover is made unique by gathering the fabric vertically at the center front of the seat to create a graceful line to the skirt. A tie is placed at the end of the gathered section for emphasis.

Back: The same vertical line of gathered fabric is created on the face of the back cover of this highly fitted design. Any design that calls for tight gathers should be made of lightweight fabric that exhibits superior drapability.

Seat: The seat of your chair is a perfect space to center fabric with a large motif. In this design, the central pattern is placed on the chair seat and it is edged with a tightly gathered skirt. A double ruffle separates the two sections of the cover.

Back: The motif centered on the seat is also featured at the center of the inner back panel of this cover. A double ruffle trims the print fabric and a gathered section of fabric that matches the skirt wraps around the chair back.

Seat: This design is a classic French-inspired chair cover with a short knife-pleated ruffle at the edge. Extra-long fabric ties wind around the chair legs multiple times before ending in bows tied at the ends.

Back: The cover for this chair back consists of two panels trimmed with a smaller version of the knife-pleated ruffle used in the skirt. Fabric ties connect the front panel to the back panel and secure it in place by tying together at the back.

Seat: Special attention should be paid to pattern matching, especially when joining flat skirts to a flat seat cover. Welting inserted in the seams can help to cover any flaws in your pattern match.

Back: The side banding of a round seat back is particularly hard to match and one side of the pattern will be upside down as it runs up and then down the far side of the round back. Keep this in mind when choosing your fabrics.

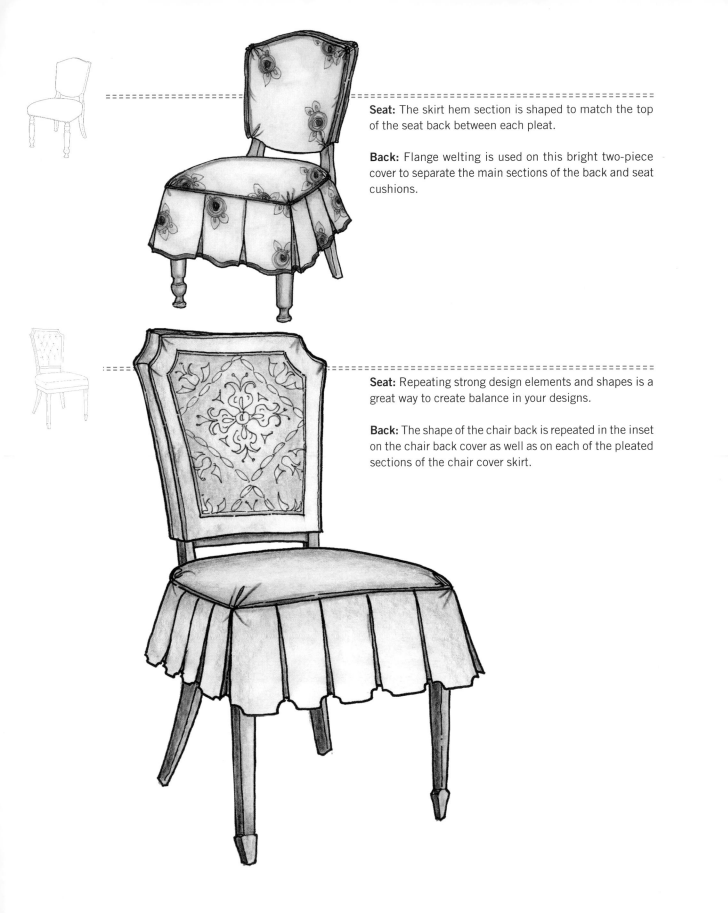

Seat: The skirt hem section is shaped to match the top of the seat back between each pleat.

Back: Flange welting is used on this bright two-piece cover to separate the main sections of the back and seat cushions.

Seat: Repeating strong design elements and shapes is a great way to create balance in your designs.

Back: The shape of the chair back is repeated in the inset on the chair back cover as well as on each of the pleated sections of the chair cover skirt.

ONE-PIECE
CHAIR COVERS

Dining chairs have long been a favorite candidate for full-length slipcovers. They can range from very simple loose-fitting throws to highly tailored multilayered designs that fit the chair like a glove.

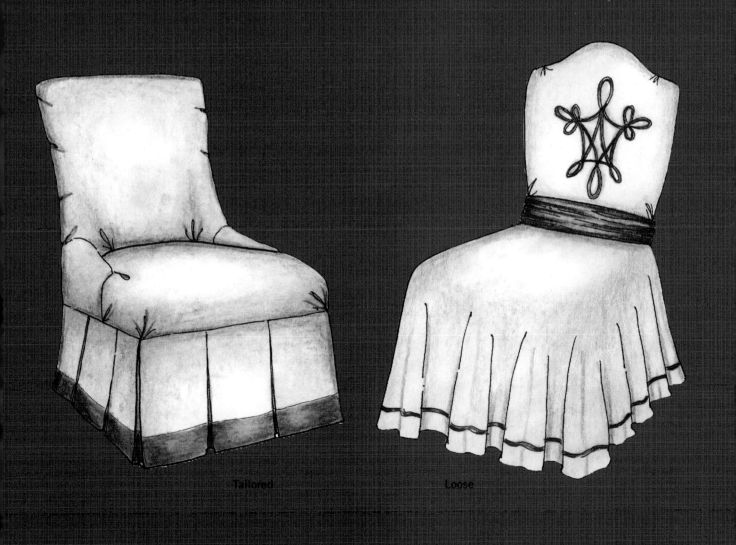

Tailored   Loose

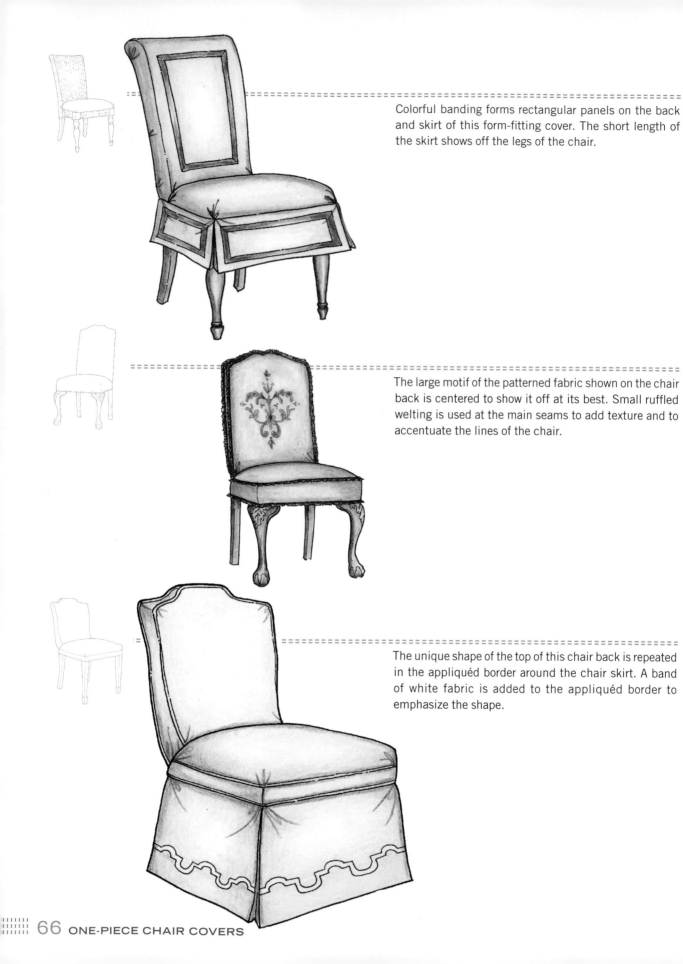

Colorful banding forms rectangular panels on the back and skirt of this form-fitting cover. The short length of the skirt shows off the legs of the chair.

The large motif of the patterned fabric shown on the chair back is centered to show it off at its best. Small ruffled welting is used at the main seams to add texture and to accentuate the lines of the chair.

The unique shape of the top of this chair back is repeated in the appliquéd border around the chair skirt. A band of white fabric is added to the appliquéd border to emphasize the shape.

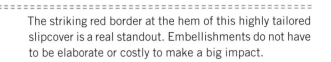

The striking red border at the hem of this highly tailored slipcover is a real standout. Embellishments do not have to be elaborate or costly to make a big impact.

The underskirt of this design is pleated at each corner and again at the inside edge of each leg. The overskirt is made of separate bordered panels that lay over the underskirt. They are sized to correspond to the pleat locations of the underskirt.

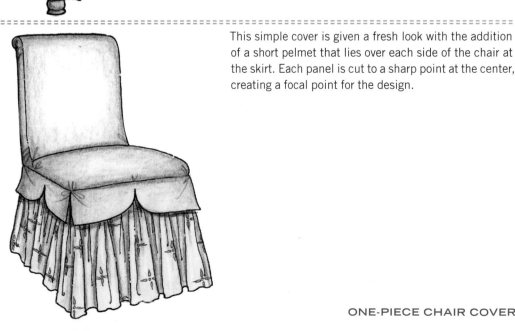

This simple cover is given a fresh look with the addition of a short pelmet that lies over each side of the chair at the skirt. Each panel is cut to a sharp point at the center, creating a focal point for the design.

The flowing skirt of this chair cover is split up the side at the arm to allow it to drape around the support post. It is closed at the opening with ties knotted into bows. The cover also splits at the back side of the chair to allow the cover to fit around the base of the arm. This type of cover requires skill and precision for a good fit.

A separate panel of fabric that is split halfway up its length is laid over the underskirt of this cover and sewn into the skirt seam. The edge of these panels at the sides of the chair hides the opening of the chair skirt necessary for the cover to fit around the arm support. It is held in place with hidden hook-and-loop tape.

Intricate detail is added to the back and hem of this loose-fitting cover with ribbon appliqué. The chair cover is held in place with the addition of a wide sash that matches the appliqué color and ties into a long bow at the back of the chair.

This cover style is best left to experts because of the detail and fitting necessary to achieve success. The detail is brought to every area of the chair including the covers for the arm pads that tie in place under the arm.

Sheer fabric is used to give a modern look to this very traditional dining chair. The sheerness of the fabric lets the beautiful lines of the chair show through while adding a new clean profile to it.

The skirt of this highly detailed design is made in three parts. First, flat panels end short with a flange welt and a scalloped border. Then a ruffled skirt is added beneath the scallop to finish it off. Separate fold-over arm covers are fitted with fabric loops at the front to allow the chair arms to be exposed.

A sharp geometric border done in a contrasting fabric brings a modern element to the back and skirt of this traditionally styled chair.

This modern wingback chair has a very simple profile that is given some added detail at the front of the arms by creating a faux-lacing effect across the face of the arm panel and down the skirt, tying in a knot at the bottom.

The subtle shape of the top rail of this chair back is repeated on the skirt but is done so upside down to reflect the shape at the top. The banding at the bottom calls attention to the shape of the hem.

This pretty chair is all dressed up in a gathered skirt with a tailored cover that leaves the carved detail at the center back exposed. The cover openings at both sides of the back are tied closed with a series of bows.

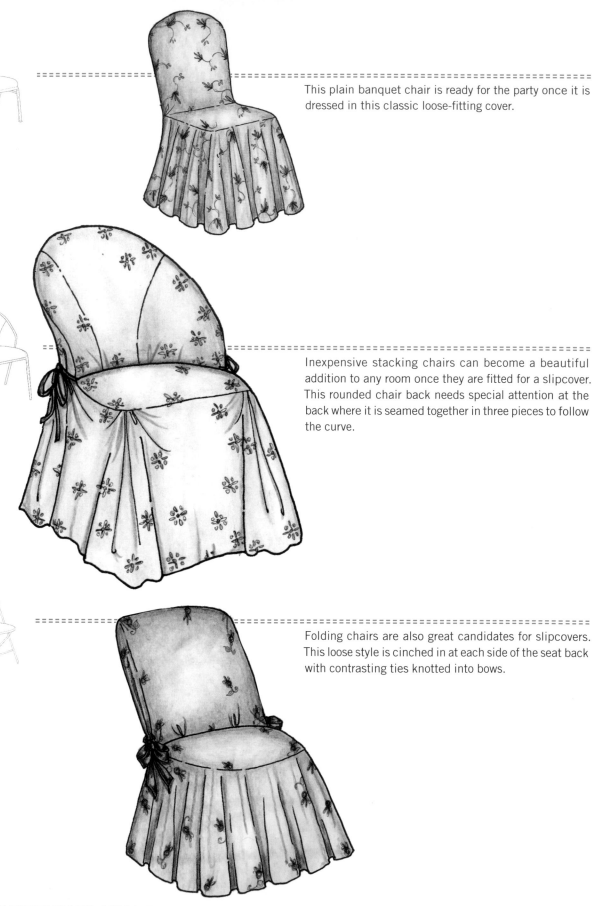

This plain banquet chair is ready for the party once it is dressed in this classic loose-fitting cover.

Inexpensive stacking chairs can become a beautiful addition to any room once they are fitted for a slipcover. This rounded chair back needs special attention at the back where it is seamed together in three pieces to follow the curve.

Folding chairs are also great candidates for slipcovers. This loose style is cinched in at each side of the seat back with contrasting ties knotted into bows.

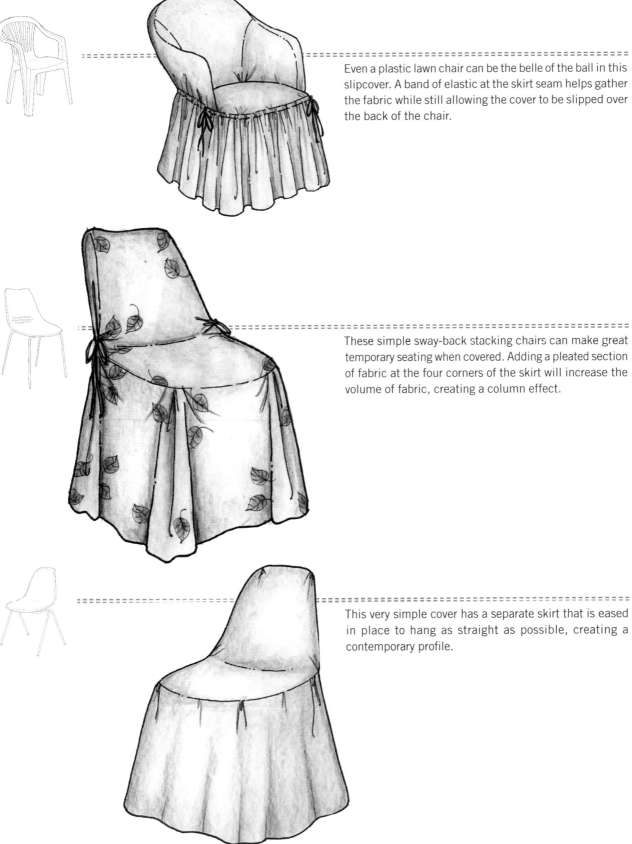

Even a plastic lawn chair can be the belle of the ball in this slipcover. A band of elastic at the skirt seam helps gather the fabric while still allowing the cover to be slipped over the back of the chair.

These simple sway-back stacking chairs can make great temporary seating when covered. Adding a pleated section of fabric at the four corners of the skirt will increase the volume of fabric, creating a column effect.

This very simple cover has a separate skirt that is eased in place to hang as straight as possible, creating a contemporary profile.

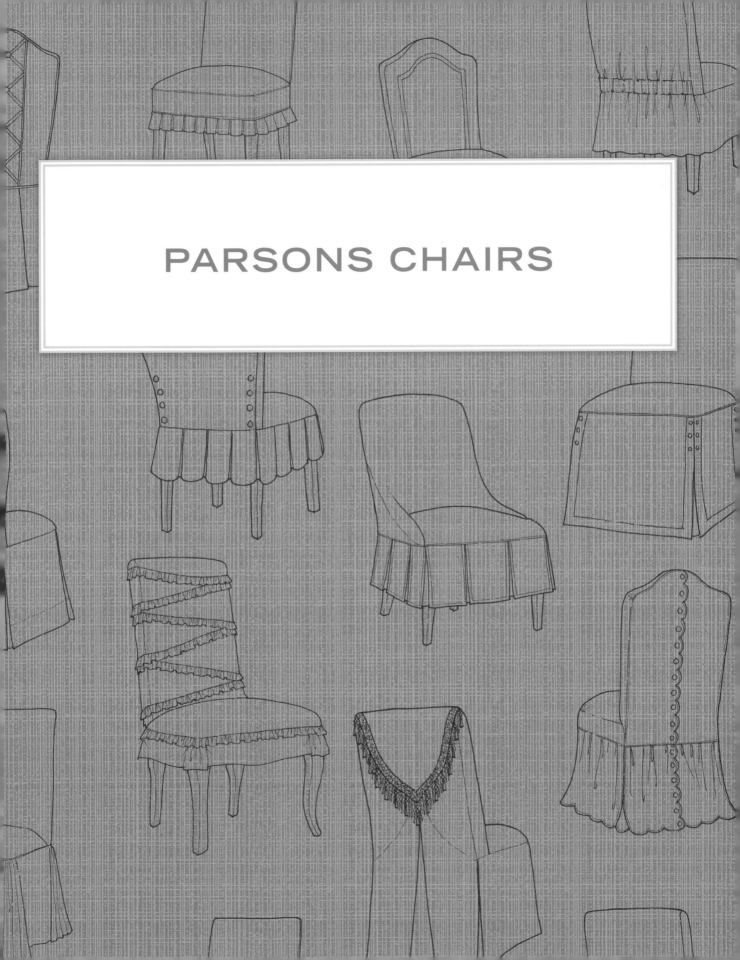

PARSONS CHAIRS

A Parsons chair is a dining or task chair that has a fully upholstered back and seat. It may also have fully upholstered legs, although some have wood or even iron legs. This type of chair is fairly easy to slipcover due to the lack of exposed wood elements and its simple styling.

Wood Legs   Upholstered Legs

Parsons chairs with fully upholstered legs should be covered with a slipcover design that includes a full-length skirt in order to obscure the existing fabric on the chair's legs.

A Parsons chair with wood legs can accommodate a slipcover with a short or mid-length skirt that exposes the wood legs.

Parsons chairs are commonly used as dining chairs or task chairs and as such are seen both from the front and back. This means that special attention should be given to the design of the back panel of the chair. Most Parsons chairs have a relatively flat back that can serve as a base for decorative embellishment.

In this chapter, you will find two sections. The first section shows common slipcover designs that highlight specific design elements that are seen from the front of the chair.

In the second section, you will see chairs shown from the back, highlighting different methods of embellishment as well as creative ways to incorporate a back closure of the chair into the design.

PARSONS CHAIRS
FRONT VIEWS

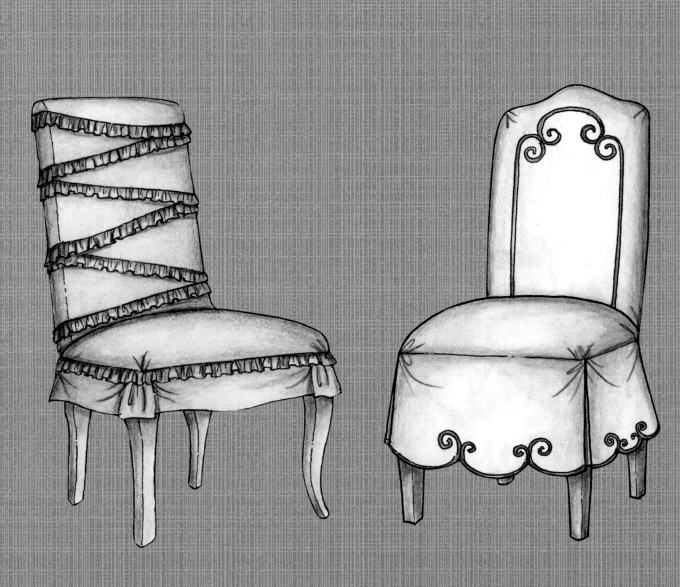

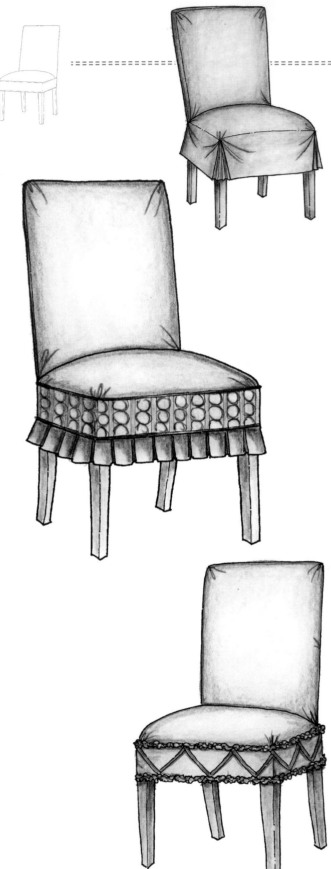

This short cover has a simple design that creates a modern profile. Double pleats are placed at all four corners of the chair skirt to add volume to the skirt and visual interest.

Careful fabric selection creates a vibrant cover for this chair. The flat panel area above the pleated edge is made using a bright vertical-striped fabric. When constructed, the pattern of the stripe imparts a highly custom look to this design.

A short, ruffled, ribbon trim is used as welting on the bottom band of this cover. Flat ribbon is added in a zigzag pattern along the face of the banding to create visual interest.

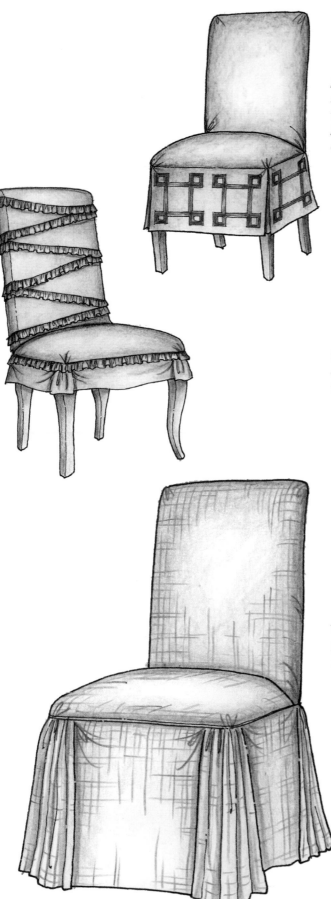

Appliquéing ribbon on your cover is a great way to make a large design statement for a small cost. On the skirt of this cover, a series of squares create a modern design. Adjust the size and quantities of the motifs to fit properly on the more narrow side panels.

Stripes of short ruffles crisscross over the inside and outside back of this adorable cover with a final row around the base of the skirt.

Volume is created in this slipcover's skirt by shirring or gathering the fabric at the four corners of the seat. The remainder of the skirt is left flat.

Inserting small pleats at each corner of the separate banding at the chair seat of this cover makes the skirt appear to be held together by the contrasting ties at each pleat.

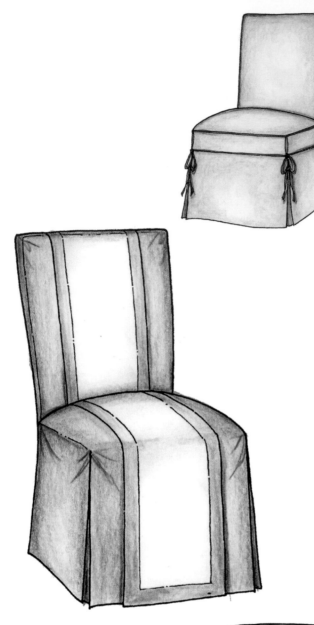

The seat and front panel of this sleek design are one piece of fabric with no seam at the face of the chair. The contrasting, bordered banner is attached to the cover at the inner back and seat but hangs free from the face of the chair skirt.

The white border of this tailored chair skirt is given a pop of color with rows of contrasting buttons at each corner.

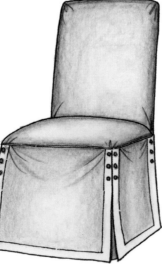

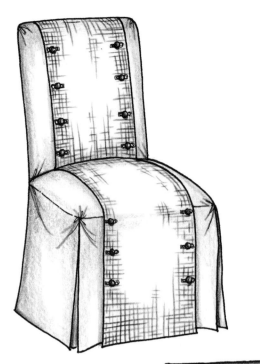

The center panel running down the face and skirt of his cover can be made as a completely separate piece from the main cover. It is buttoned in place and can be made reversible to add versatility to the plain cover. When using buttons on the inner back of a chair cover, be sure they are as flat as possible so they do not cause discomfort to those using the chair.

Simple tucks made in this slipcover skirt create a wonderful texture and sense of movement on an otherwise plain cover. The skirt sections are made as separate sections and a matching corner section is applied underneath.

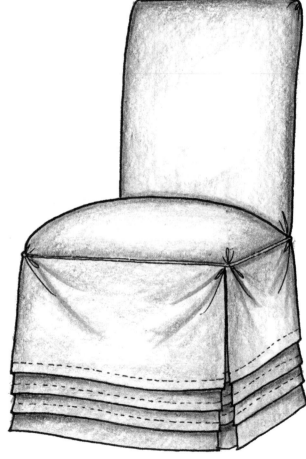

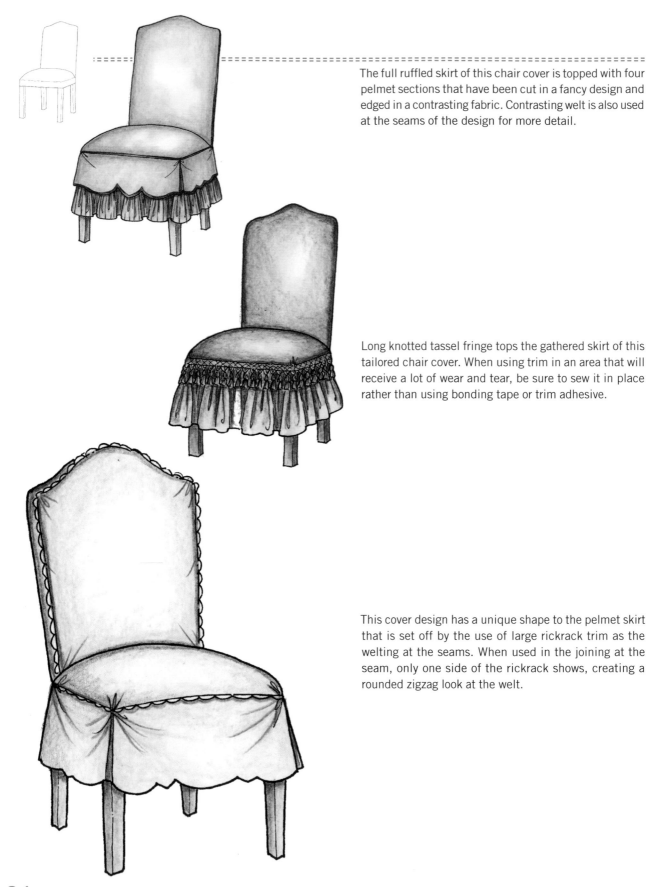

The full ruffled skirt of this chair cover is topped with four pelmet sections that have been cut in a fancy design and edged in a contrasting fabric. Contrasting welt is also used at the seams of the design for more detail.

Long knotted tassel fringe tops the gathered skirt of this tailored chair cover. When using trim in an area that will receive a lot of wear and tear, be sure to sew it in place rather than using bonding tape or trim adhesive.

This cover design has a unique shape to the pelmet skirt that is set off by the use of large rickrack trim as the welting at the seams. When used in the joining at the seam, only one side of the rickrack shows, creating a rounded zigzag look at the welt.

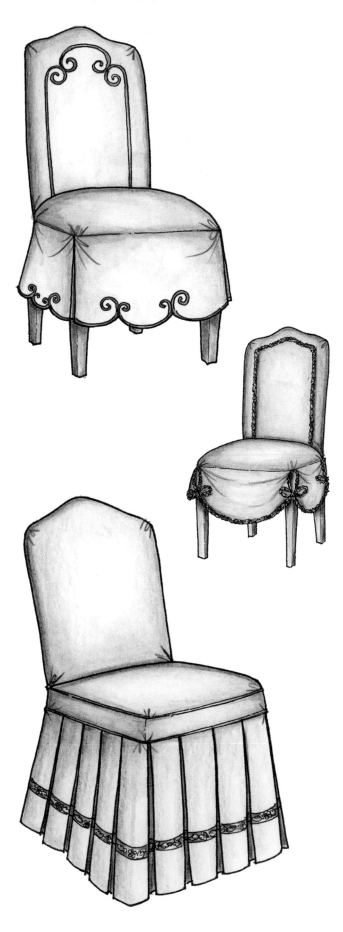

Intricate patterns are created by applying contrasting gimp in scallops and curls at the inside back panel and skirt hem in this design. Test your gimp for appropriate flexibility before trying this method.

This design also uses short, looped ribbon ruffle trim to create a textured border at the inside back panel. It is also used to edge the chair skirt and loops up and out at each corner to create a striking fleur-de-lis motif.

When planning to use a design that incorporates box pleats such as in this slipcover, test your fabric's creasing ability by pressing a few pleats in a sample to be sure it will hold its shape over time.

The scallops of this overskirt correspond to the pleats in the underskirt. Each corner is embellished with small contrasting buttons for a fun touch.

This chair cover features a contrasting insert at the center of the inside chair back. This is a great area to use a fabric with a large pattern motif. The joining seams are covered with ribbon or decorative tape.

Short, looped ribbon ruffle trim is used on this cover to create the detail on inside back panel. It is also used around the perimeter of the seat. Matching looped ribbon fringe is added to the bottom of the cover.

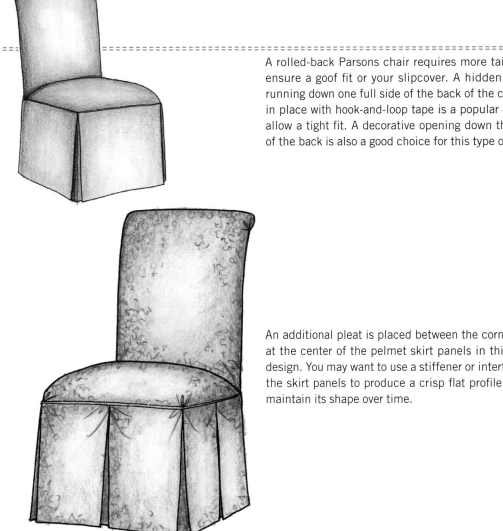

A rolled-back Parsons chair requires more tailoring to ensure a goof fit or your slipcover. A hidden opening running down one full side of the back of the chair held in place with hook-and-loop tape is a popular option to allow a tight fit. A decorative opening down the center of the back is also a good choice for this type of chair.

An additional pleat is placed between the corner pleats at the center of the pelmet skirt panels in this classic design. You may want to use a stiffener or interfacing on the skirt panels to produce a crisp flat profile that will maintain its shape over time.

When designing a cover with a full gathered skirt, avoid heavyweight fabrics that will bunch up at the seat cover seam. Mid- to lightweight fabrics work best for this type of look.

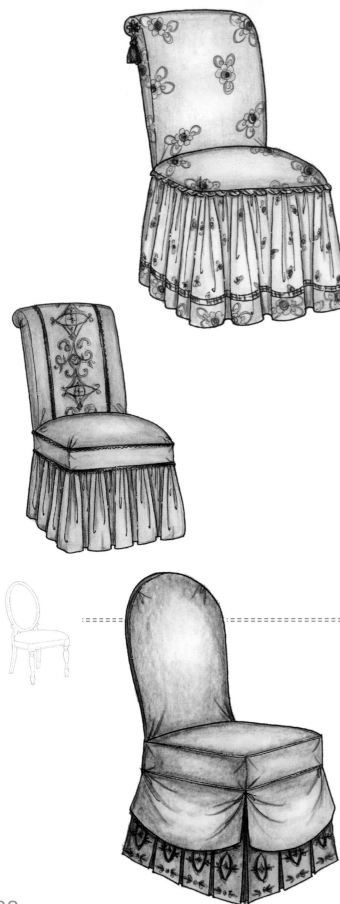

Attention to detail makes this slipcover design stand out. A small, contrasting, scalloped edge is inserted at the skirt seam and a matching band of fabric separates the main skirt fabric from a wide border at the bottom. A key tassel that matches the edging fabric is placed at the center of the rolled side of the back.

The center panel of this skirted slipcover is used to display the large motif of a patterned fabric. The rest of the cover is made of a solid fabric. Decorative trim separates the main sections of the chair and the back panel from one another.

Relaxed panels top the crisp pleats of this slipcover's overskirt. Small pleats are tucked in at each corner of the panels to add a small swaging droop in the panel.

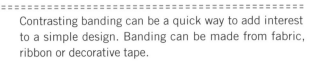

Contrasting banding can be a quick way to add interest to a simple design. Banding can be made from fabric, ribbon or decorative tape.

The center of this fun chair skirt is gathered to create volume and give the cover a swaged profile. A placket is sewn over the gathered seam and embellished with buttons. The back seams of the skirt are also gathered up slightly to allow the swags to follow around to the chair front.

A tube casing is sewn into each side seam of the overskirt of this cover so that a fabric tie can be attached at the seat seam and threaded through so the casing can cinch up the fabric into an accordion-pleated design.

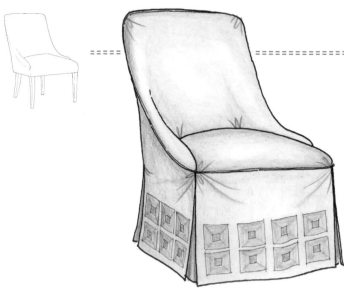

A creative use of appliqué on this chair cover gives it a fun, modern look not usually associated with that technique. Two color patches similar to quilt squares are placed in symmetrical rows and repeated around the skirt of the cover. These squares can be sewn on or applied with bonding tape or fusible webbing.

A thin contrasting border is applied to the edges of each separate panel of the overskirt on this cover, creating a bold geometric design. An underskirt covers the chair frame and adds support to the individual panels of the overskirt.

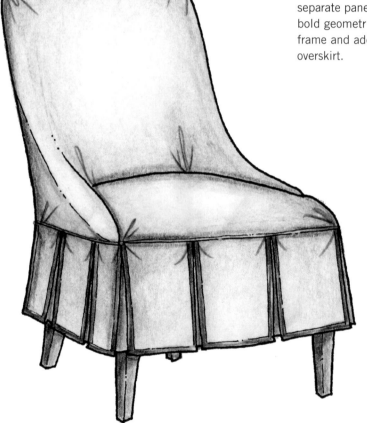

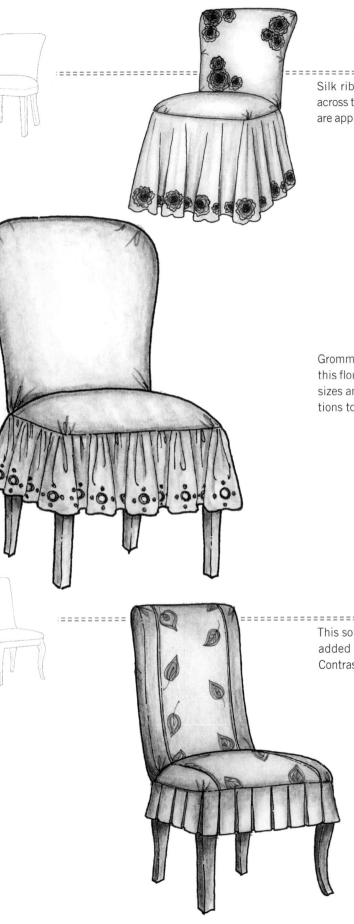

Silk ribbon roses made in different sizes are scattered across the back of this cover. Large and small ribbon roses are applied in a line at the hem, creating a fabulous border.

Grommets are used to create a fun design on the hem of this flouncy skirt. They come in many shapes, colors and sizes and can be used in an endless number of combinations to create a truly unique look for your design.

This solid-colored cover is embellished with a bold print added in a center insert on the chair back and seat. Contrasting welting set the two areas apart.

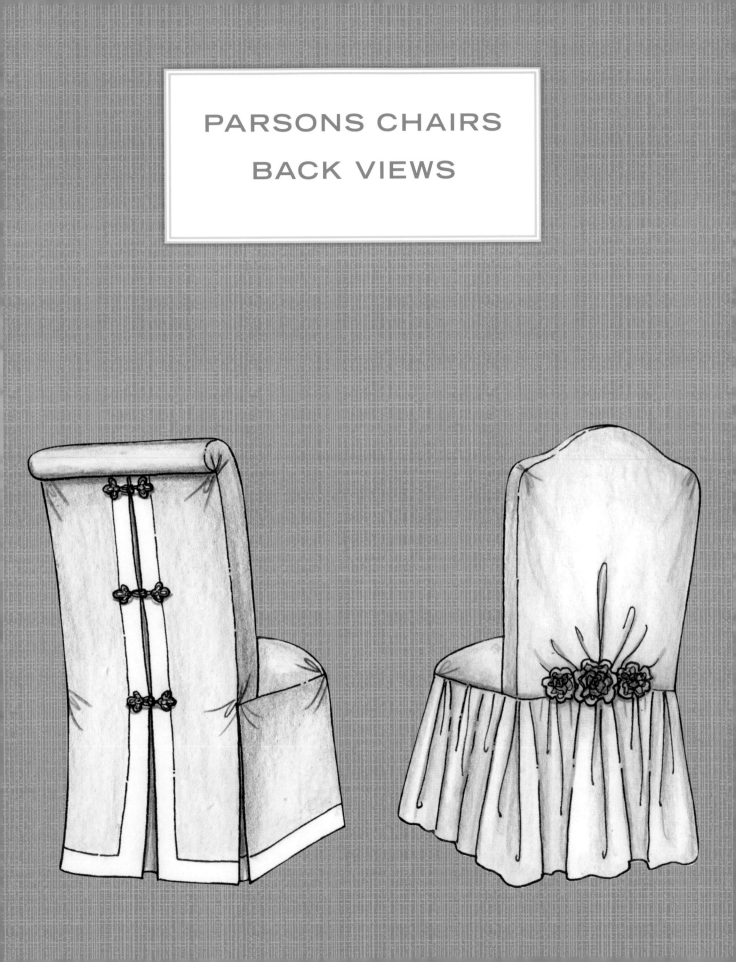

PARSONS CHAIRS
BACK VIEWS

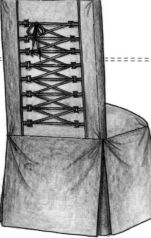

Inspired by a vintage corset, this elaborate design uses a series of tabs fitted with metal buckles that are threaded with one very long tie that crisscrosses over the back of the chair and ties at the top. The contrasting panel at the middle of the back serves as a backdrop for the crisscross detail.

Fabric loops are sewn into the seam at the back panel of this cover and a long tie is threaded through the loops and tied at the bottom, creating a laced effect. Chair tassels are attached to the ends of the fabric tie.

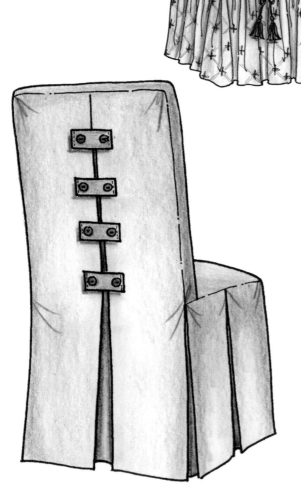

A contrasting fabric is used for the inside pleat sections of this slipcover's skirt, creating a strong vertical component to the design. Wide horizontal tabs done in the contrasting fabric are buttoned along the center back pleat to hold it in place. The conflicting horizontal and vertical lines of the design bring it into balance.

Leather straps are fitted with belt buckles on the back of this fun masculine cover. Matching leather welting carries the theme to the rest of the cover.

This pretty cover starts with a shirred panel at the back that is flanked by two flat back sections that fold over it at the center. A contrasting border and bow at the center of the back serve to divide the two separate textures.

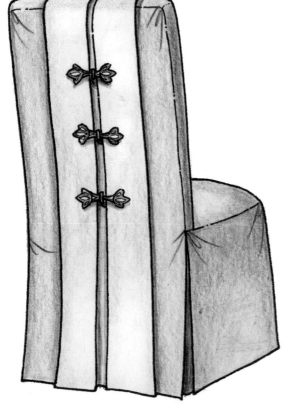

In many cases, the back opening is best left hidden by running it up the side of the chair and securing the two pieces with hidden hook-and-loop tape. This allows you to get more creative in the back panel design as with this cover. Here, a center back panel is pleated and embellished with decorative frogs.

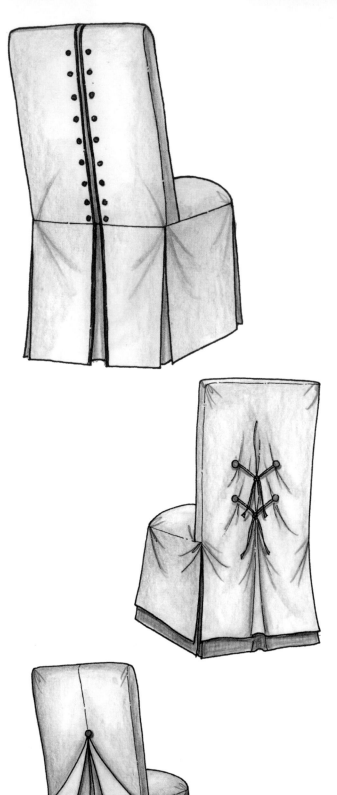

Contrasting buttons and welting create interest at the back of this simple cover. If you plan to wash your slipcovers and you are using contrasting colors that might bleed or stain one another, be sure to check them for colorfastness before construction.

The excess fabric of this loose-fitting cover is cinched in at the back panel by contrasting fabric ties that are attached with buttons at each side of the panel. The ties can be pulled in as desired for a good fit of the cover over the chair. A contrasting underskirt finishes off the design.

A tuxedo-type opening is created at the back of this chair by folding back portions of the back panel to reveal a separate underskirt with a long central pleat. The back flaps are held in place with contrasting buttons.

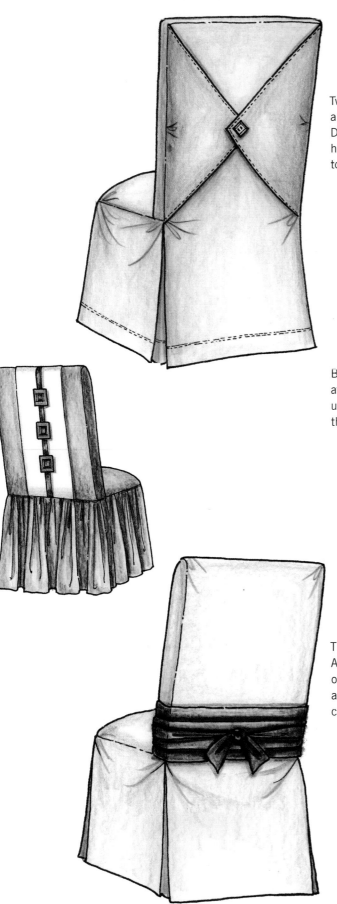

Two triangle-shaped flaps of contrasting fabric overlap and button together at the center back of this cover. Decorative topstitching is used on the panels and at the hem of the cover to create continuity and to add detail to this design.

Belt buckles are threaded through a band of fabric attached to the back of this slipcover to create a fun and unique detail. The white panel beneath the buckles shows them off and sets them apart from the rest of the cover.

This design is inspired by a traditional Japanese kimono. A wide band of contrasting fabric runs around the bottom of the chair back and a second matching tie is wrapped around the back twice and ties in place at the outside center of the chair.

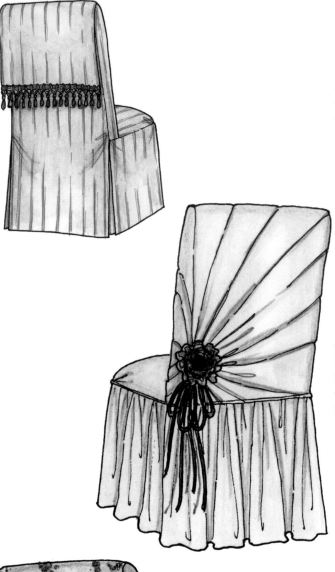

Long tassel fringe borders the shawl-style back of this tailored slipcover. The shawl section originates from the top back seam and extends separately down the back so that it hangs independently from the rest of the slipcover.

Couture fitting is required for this beautiful slipcover. Fabric is meticulously pleated and stretched across the back of this chair cover and cinched together at the side where it is embellished with a large rosette and long looping ties.

Rather than gathering excess fabric into the middle of the chair, this design pulls it to each side of the chair back and holds it in place with long tabs that button in place, creating additional volume in the width of the skirt back.

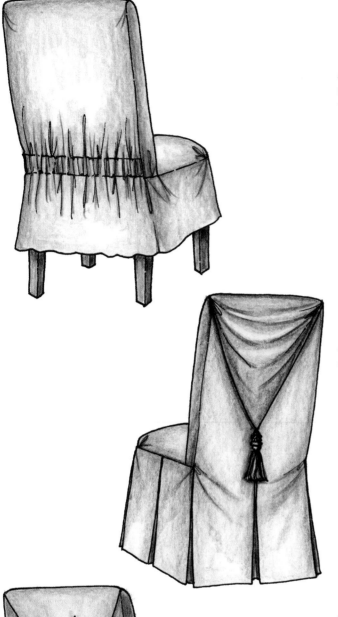

A wide casing is sewn into the lower back of this cover and elastic is threaded through it to gather up the excess fabric, creating a pleasing design element in the process.

A swaged flag or pennant hangs gracefully down the back of this slipcover, ending in a large key tassel at the center pleat of the chair skirt.

The back panel of this cover is fitted with a second separate layer of fabric that matches the skirt that is cinched in at the center and topped with a large rosette.

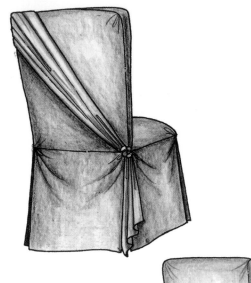

This slipcover is ready for a beauty pageant with a dramatic scarf attached at the top back corner. The scarf angles across the chair back and cascades down the side of the chair skirt. A separate fabric knot at the corner gives the scarf the appearance of being tied in place.

Simple custom details can make a big difference when designing your slipcovers. Here, the back skirt seam is given a gentle scallop that softens the look of the overall design.

A much more simple version of the crisscross detail is used on this chair cover. Contrasting straps inserted at the side seams of the cover cross over one another at the center back and are held in place by buttons.

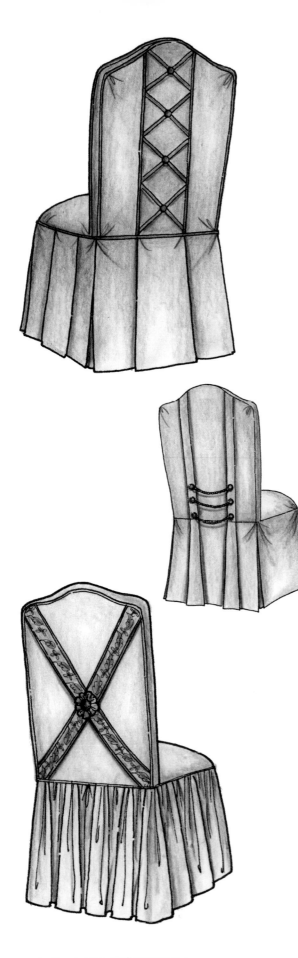

The crisscross detail on this cover is narrow and runs down the back of the chair, meeting up with the center section of the chair skirt. The four sides of the skirt are folded to create a central panel.

Inspired by a vintage lady's suit, this slipcover has two contrasting bands of fabric that lead to matching pleated sections in the skirt. Buttons on either side of the lower back are linked together with decorative chain.

Fabric with a large motif arranged in stripes can be cut to make a dramatic border. Here, a wide border is trimmed with a contrasting welt and crossed over the back of this slipcover. A rosette highlights the center of the crossed borders.

A fun faux suede shoulder and seat placket and leather buckles give this design a western flair. Contrasting faux suede finishes up the rest of the cover.

Fluffy rosettes create a focal point at the back of this cover. The rosettes also serve to disguise the elastic casing at the back that cinches in the excess fabric of the cover.

Contrasting welt and edging are a simple way to add detail and color to any plain slipcover. Self-covered buttons can add another level of dimension and style to your designs.

Layers of ruffles swoop up to a sharp point at the back of this ultra-feminine slipcover. The top layer is cut on the radius to produce a flouncy ruffle with no bulk at the seam while the skirt is a traditional gathered ruffle.

Tight scallops highlighted with contrasting welt edge this back opening that is held closed with contrasting buttons placed in each scallop. The contrasting welt continues around the skirt hem and at the back seam.

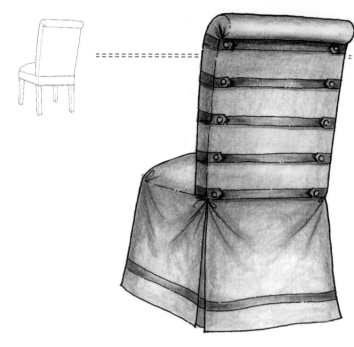

Reminiscent of a military blazer, the horizontal straps running around the back of this chair cover end in points at each side of the back panel and are buttoned in place. An additional stripe is added around the hem of the chair skirt to balance out the design.

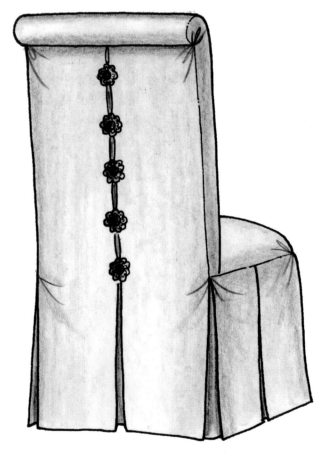

The back opening of this slipcover is held closed with hidden hook-and-loop tape. The rosettes are attached at one side and a hook and eye is used to hold them in place at the other side. The result is the illusion that the rosettes are holding the panel sections together.

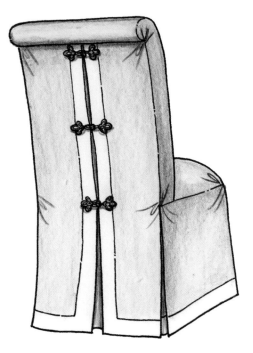

This oriental-inspired design uses decorative frogs as closures at the back panel opening. The double contrasting border running from the chair backroll down the back and around the skirt emphasizes the lines of the chair.

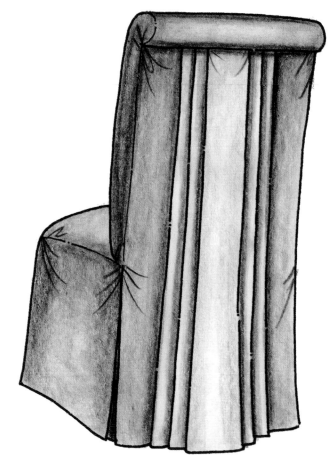

Stacked, pleated layers graduate out from the center at the back of this dramatic slipcover. Be sure to use a crisp, lightweight fabric when trying this technique to avoid creating too much bulk.

Two overlapping sections meet at the center back opening of this design and button in place. The wide contrasting border follows the graceful curve of the hem, around to the front of the skirt.

The back panel and skirt of this chair cover are constructed to open in order to fit the cover over the chair. Contrasting buttons hold the back and side panels together and hidden hook-and-loop tape connects the side sections of the skirt to the back section.

This tailored slipcover is embellished simply with two perky bows at either side of the lower back of the chair.

The excess fabric of this loose-fitting cover is cinched in at the center back with a wide band of contrasting fabric that ends in long ties and a bow.

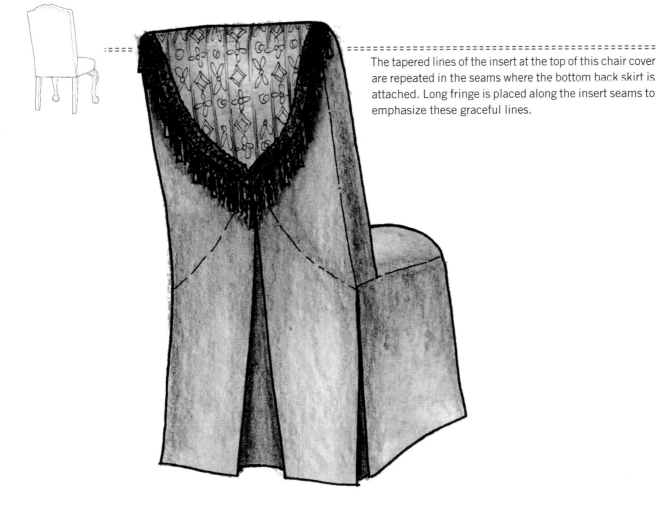

The tapered lines of the insert at the top of this chair cover are repeated in the seams where the bottom back skirt is attached. Long fringe is placed along the insert seams to emphasize these graceful lines.

CLUB CHAIRS, SETTEES AND SOFAS

Full-coverage slipcovers for club chairs, sofas and sectionals can be complicated and take a higher level of skill in planning and construction due to the exacting nature of their fit. They are bulky, with multiple yards of fabric to handle, and are harder to sew.

The style of your cover will be dictated by the lines and design of your piece of furniture. There are several key design choices that you can make to customize the design of your cover.

Skirt Style

Welting Style

Embellishments

Take a cue from the many skirts, welting, trim and embellishment details shown in previous chapters of this book to design your unique cover.

ARM STYLES

Sofas and club chairs come in a wide variety of styles with the design of the arm being a key component that defines the look of the whole piece.

The design of a slipcover for these pieces of furniture will also be defined by the shape of the arm and the limitations of ways to cover it. Most pieces will have either a full arm or a recessed arm.

Full Arms

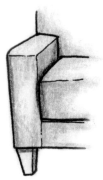

Tuxedo

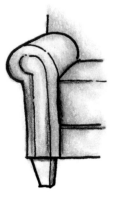

Roll with Placket

Gathered Roll

Deco

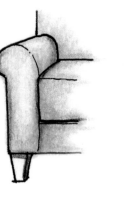

Roll

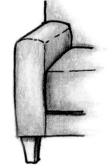

Rounded Tuxedo

CUSHIONS

Most furniture will fall into one of two seating categories:

Recessed Arms

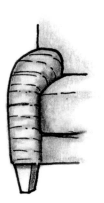

English

Tuxedo

Victorian

Roll

English

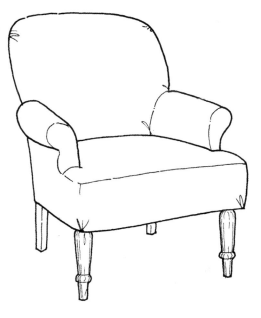

Fixed cushion seat and fixed cushion back

Loose cushion seat and loose cushion back

SEAT CUSHION STYLES

The three most common seat cushion styles used on upholstered furnishings are boxed cushions, center seam cushions and T-cushions.

Boxed

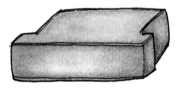

Center Seam

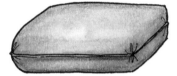

T-Cushions

Boxed Cushion

This type of cushion can take on any shape but is predominantly square or rectangular. It has three separate surfaces, a top face, a bottom face and a side band. The term *boxed* refers to the side band of fabric that runs around the perimeter of the cushion between the top face and bottom face. The sections of fabric can be sewn directly together or welting can be inserted between them.

Center Seam Cushion

This cushion has only two separate surfaces; a top face and a bottom face. The two pieces are sewn together, creating one center seam. Height and interior volume are created by adding pleats to the four corners. The two layers of fabric can be sewn directly together or welting can be inserted between them. Welting can add strength to the cushion.

T-Cushion

Similar to a boxed cushion in construction, this cushion has two face sides and a side band. It is shaped like the letter T to accommodate the recessed arms of a chair or sofa.

ADDING A SKIRT

The skirt of a slipcover is attached to the rest of the cover in one of two locations.

On a cover for a piece of furniture with loose seat cushions, the skirt is attached just below the loose cushion at the seam of the seat decking.

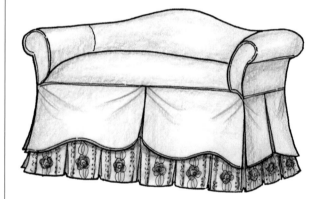

BASIC SKIRT STYLES

While there are hundreds of possible skirt designs shown in this book, most of them will fall into a few main categories.

Pelmet

Gathered

Pleated

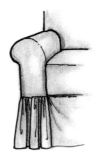

Gathered Corners

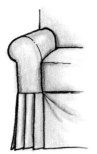

Pleated Corners

Layered

DESIGNING FOR DIFFERENT SHAPES AND SIZES

The basic design of a slipcover for a fully upholstered piece of furniture remains the same whether it is fitted for a chair, a love seat, a sofa or a sectional. The core elements of the design are adjusted to fit the size and shape of the furniture.

The example below shows a basic tailored slipcover with boxed seat cushions, center seam back cushions, and a pelmet skirt with pleats at the four corners and at the seat cushion points.

Club Chair

Settee or Love Seat

Sofa

CLUB CHAIRS

Club chairs are fully upholstered on the back arms and seat and have either attached or loose seat or back cushions. The legs or feet of the chair are sometimes left exposed.

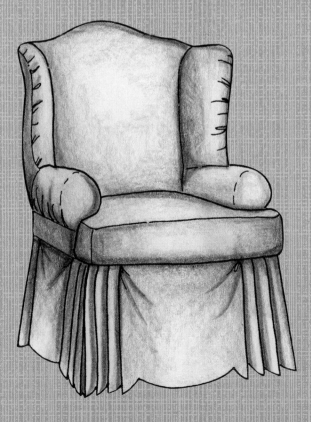

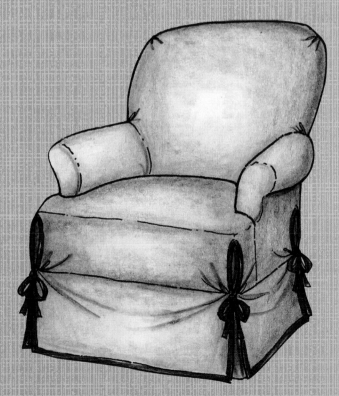

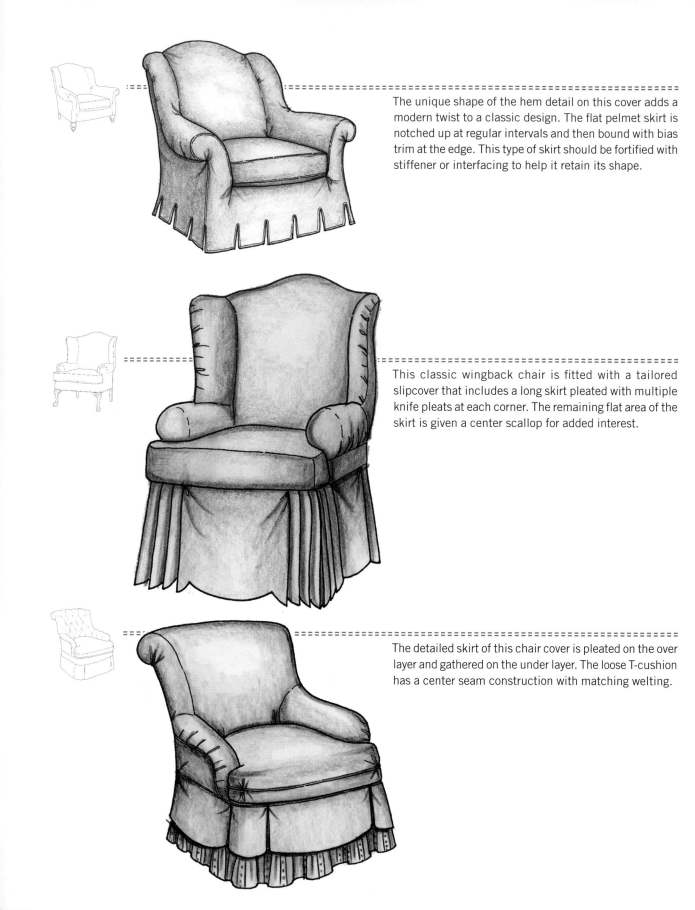

The unique shape of the hem detail on this cover adds a modern twist to a classic design. The flat pelmet skirt is notched up at regular intervals and then bound with bias trim at the edge. This type of skirt should be fortified with stiffener or interfacing to help it retain its shape.

This classic wingback chair is fitted with a tailored slipcover that includes a long skirt pleated with multiple knife pleats at each corner. The remaining flat area of the skirt is given a center scallop for added interest.

The detailed skirt of this chair cover is pleated on the over layer and gathered on the under layer. The loose T-cushion has a center seam construction with matching welting.

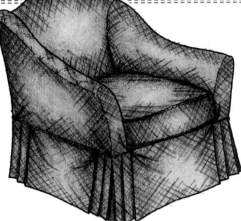

Knife pleats, folded out towards the sides of the chair, are lined up in threes at each corner of this chair's slipcover. This creates a stacked effect on the skirt with the central panel of each side of the cover standing out on top of the rest.

Gentle scallops are created on the skirt of this chair cover by applying short pleated ruffles on the face only. The ruffles stop at the pleat crease to avoid creating excess bulk in the pleat and to maintain the flow of the line of the scallops across the skirt. The hem is slightly scalloped and is trimmed in the same short pleats.

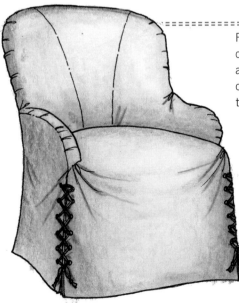

Faux leather laces hold the open panels of the front chair cover in place. They are threaded through small grommets at each side of the skirt opening. The inside back of the cover is seamed in three pieces to follow the curve of the seat back.

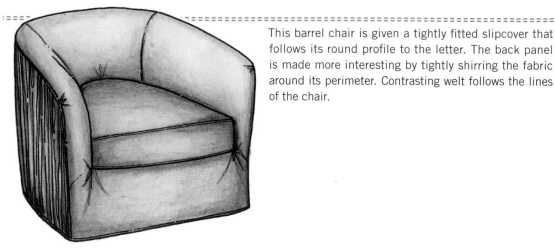

This barrel chair is given a tightly fitted slipcover that follows its round profile to the letter. The back panel is made more interesting by tightly shirring the fabric around its perimeter. Contrasting welt follows the lines of the chair.

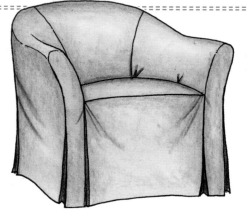

Long, crisp pleats are placed at each side of the arm panels in this sleek design, creating a subtle flair in the skirt. Two additional pleats are placed at the bottom of the back seams.

Three layers of different-colored fabrics are stacked on top of one another in short, medium and full lengths to make up the skirt design of this cover.

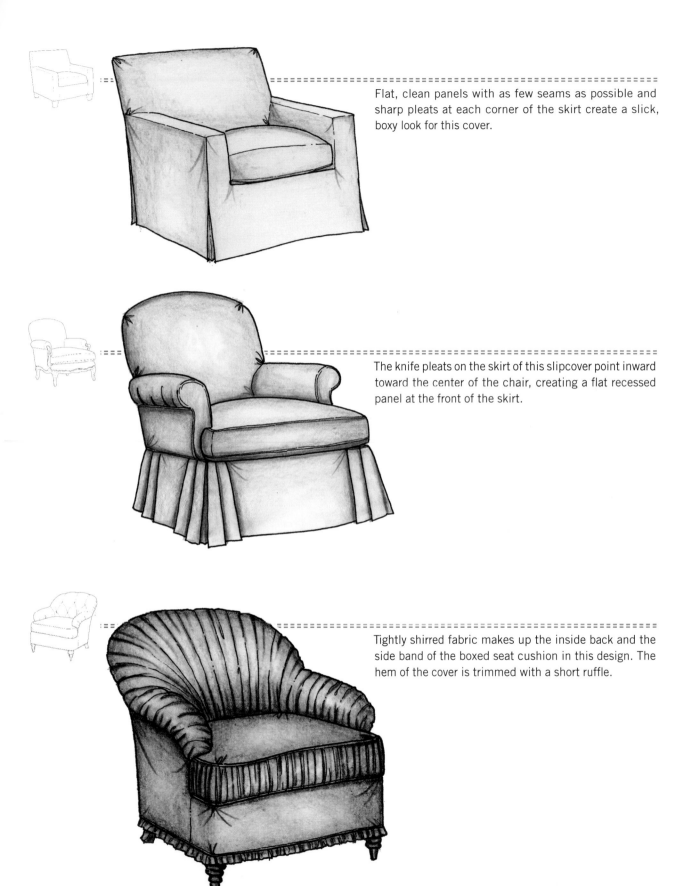

Flat, clean panels with as few seams as possible and sharp pleats at each corner of the skirt create a slick, boxy look for this cover.

The knife pleats on the skirt of this slipcover point inward toward the center of the chair, creating a flat recessed panel at the front of the skirt.

Tightly shirred fabric makes up the inside back and the side band of the boxed seat cushion in this design. The hem of the cover is trimmed with a short ruffle.

BERGÈRES

===============================

*B*ergère is a French term that describes an armchair that has an exposed wooden frame with portions of the chair covered in upholstery. This type of chair has long been a favorite piece to adorn with a slipcover both to protect the chair's upholstery and its exposed wooden frame.

Depending on the style of the chair, it can be covered in one-piece or two-piece slipcovers. Great attention to detail must be paid to fitting due to the many ins and outs of the chair's frame.

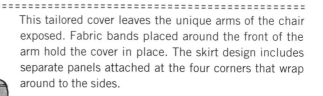

This tailored cover leaves the unique arms of the chair exposed. Fabric bands placed around the front of the arm hold the cover in place. The skirt design includes separate panels attached at the four corners that wrap around to the sides.

Flat panels of fabric fold over the arms of this chair, leaving the arms and front legs exposed. The arm panels are scooped out to show as much of the wood frame as possible while still covering the upholstery on the chair.

Banding has long been a classic element used to embellish slipcovers and chairs. The interior bands on the back and skirt reinforce the undulating lines of the chair frame. The banding fabric is repeated in the pleated underskirt.

This ultra-feminine slipcover is adorned with an accordion swaged overskirt that is embellished with ribbon flowers at the two front corners. The loose seat cushion and the overskirt are done in the same fabric so they appear to be once piece while the rest of the cover is made of a contrasting fabric

Large fabric-covered buttons in a contrasting color are used to embellish each scallop of the undulating hem on the skirt of this cover.

A peek-a-boo opening is left at the top of the back rail of this large bergère to expose the pretty carved detail at the middle of the back. The application of long bullion fringe gives this design the appearance of having a skirt.

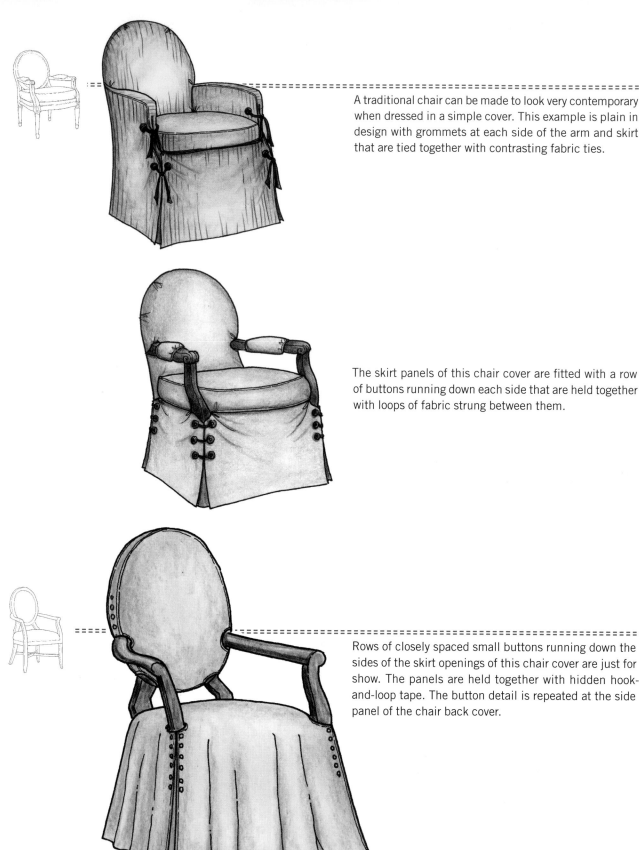

A traditional chair can be made to look very contemporary when dressed in a simple cover. This example is plain in design with grommets at each side of the arm and skirt that are tied together with contrasting fabric ties.

The skirt panels of this chair cover are fitted with a row of buttons running down each side that are held together with loops of fabric strung between them.

Rows of closely spaced small buttons running down the sides of the skirt openings of this chair cover are just for show. The panels are held together with hidden hook-and-loop tape. The button detail is repeated at the side panel of the chair back cover.

A short scalloped welt borders the skirt of this cover as well as the arm covers. The matching arm covers wrap around the padded portion of the arm and are held in place with hook-and-loop tape.

Flat welting is used on this cover in the traditional French manor with the corners pleated to ease around the curves. A double layer of short pleats borders the edge of the back cover and the seat skirt.

Flat welting is sometimes called French welt. It is a classic embellishment on traditional slipcovers. The welt runs flat along the seams of the cover and is pleated as it rounds the curves and corners of the cover.

The skirt of this cover is gathered tightly at the two front corners, creating volume in an otherwise flat skirt. The carved detail at the top rail is left exposed by cutting a scallop at the top of the cover and binding it with welting.

This cover design is simple in its construction with a flat rectangle that folds over the back and a cross-shaped panel that lies over the seat and folds down to form a skirt. The panel is held in place with long ties trimmed with decorative beads.

SLIPPER CHAIRS

==

Fitting covers to chairs with radius backs can be tricky. The back must be made up of pie-shaped pieces that seam together to follow the curve of the back. The back of this cover requires six separate pieces to manage the interior curve of the chair back.

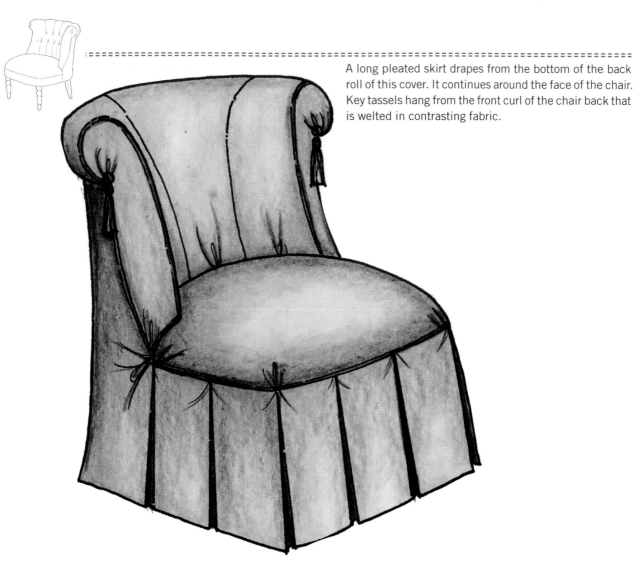

A long pleated skirt drapes from the bottom of the back roll of this cover. It continues around the face of the chair. Key tassels hang from the front curl of the chair back that is welted in contrasting fabric.

Rosettes are placed on the inside back of this cover in a corresponding pattern to the tufting on the upholstery below. This is a great way to deal with the pattern of the tufting showing through the cover. Matching rosettes also run along the skirt seam.

Double rows of contrasting box-pleated ruffles embellish a placket that runs down the inside and outside back as well as the skirt of this design.

BARSTOOLS

Barstool slipcovers are essentially designed and sewn the same as other chair covers and chair pads although they do have a few specific guidelines that should be followed.

Barstool slipcovers should not have full-length skirts. Plenty of clearance should be given between the skirt of the cover and the rungs at the bottom of the barstool meant to support the user's feet.

Swivel barstools should not have long skirts that may bunch up or twist.

Swivel barstools should not use ties that would inhibit the swivel action of the seat.

Backless barstools may need hidden support for the cover that holds the cover onto the stool under the seat.

This vintage-style barstool is dressed up with a cute skirted cover with long scallops trimmed in contrasting banding and matching buttons.

A slightly scalloped, box-pleated skirt is embellished with pointed tabs folded down from the seat top and buttoned in place.

The flouncy gathered skirt of this barstool cover is edged in a brightly striped border and a double-sided ruffle. Matching welting separated the skirt from the seat top.

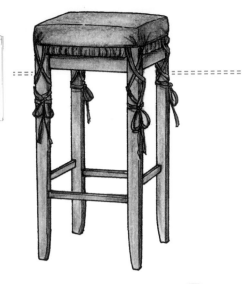

A simple boxed seat cushion is attached to this rush seat barstool with very long ties that wind around the four legs of the stool.

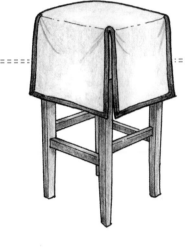

A fitted seat cover holds this slipcover in place while a simple overskirt rimmed in a contrasting banding folds down over the sides of the barstool.

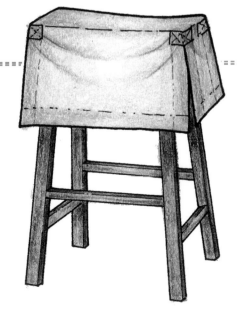

When covering a backless stool, you may need to add a couple of security straps to your design. They run underneath the seat and join together at the center with hook-and-loop tape.

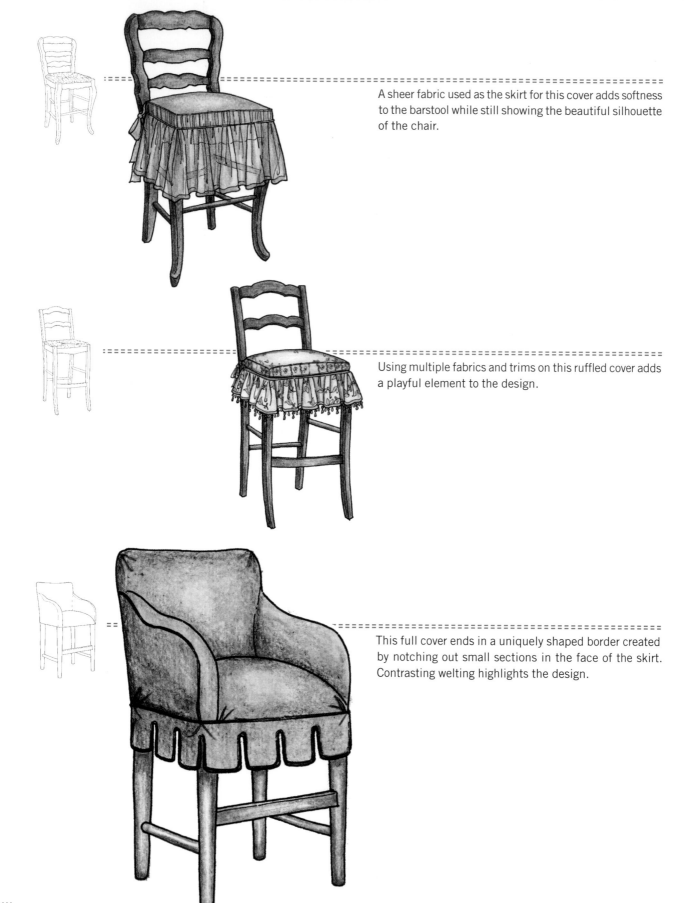

A sheer fabric used as the skirt for this cover adds softness to the barstool while still showing the beautiful silhouette of the chair.

Using multiple fabrics and trims on this ruffled cover adds a playful element to the design.

This full cover ends in a uniquely shaped border created by notching out small sections in the face of the skirt. Contrasting welting highlights the design.

Buttoned-on straps create an interesting pattern on this full cover. The straps at the back are functional, holding the openings of the cover closed, while the front straps are purely decorative.

This plain cover is given a shot of color in the underskirt that barely peaks out from under the rest of the cover.

This two-piece cover has a tufted back cushion and a pelmet skirt with gathering at the four corners. The slight peak in the pelmet panels adds a graceful note to the design.

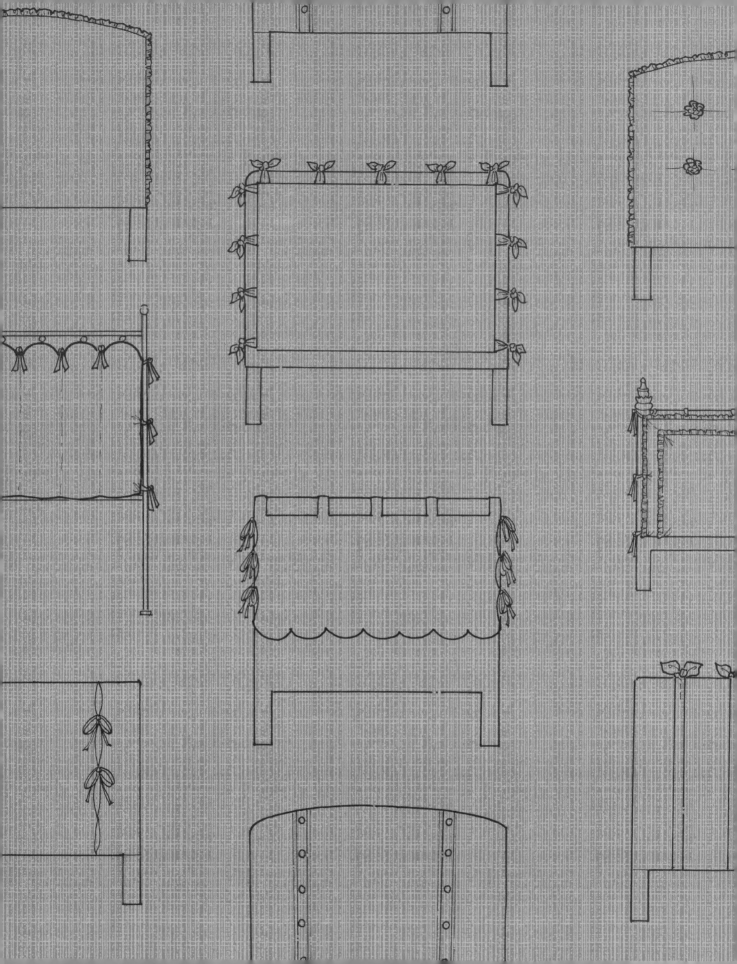

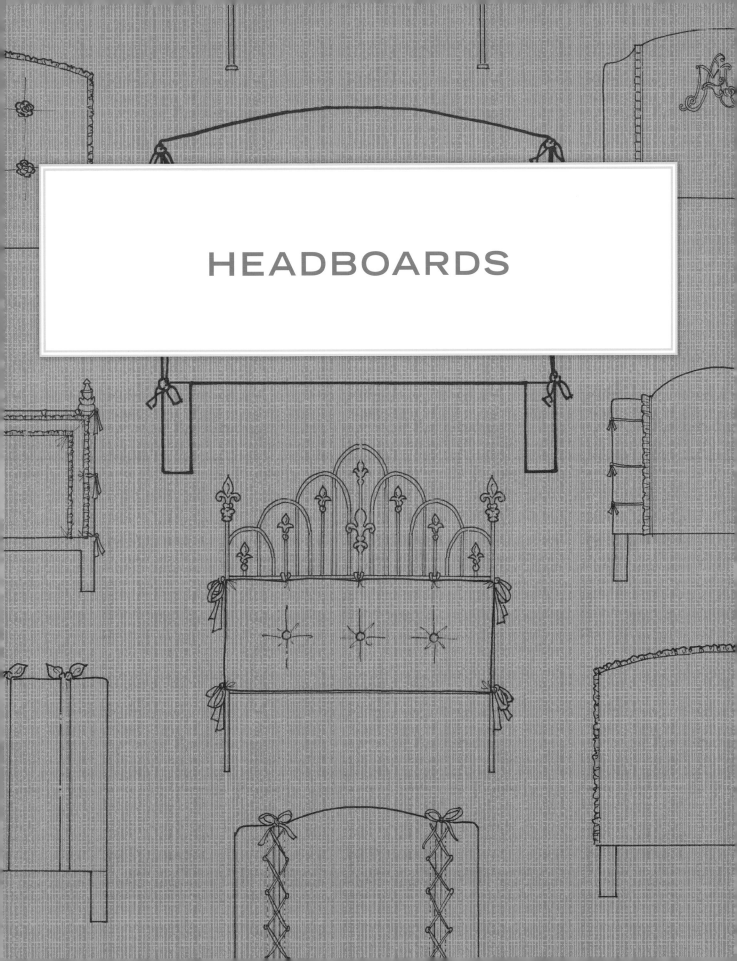

HEADBOARDS

C overing a headboard with a slipcover makes sense for many reasons.

Slipcovers can easily transform the color and style of your old headboard and give your room a brand-new look.

A partial slipcover or dust cover can protect the expensive fabric of your headboard from wear and tear and can be removed easily to be washed.

Padding can be added to your slipcover to provide additional comfort to a hard surface headboard.

Slipcovers can give your bedroom a quick seasonal design change.

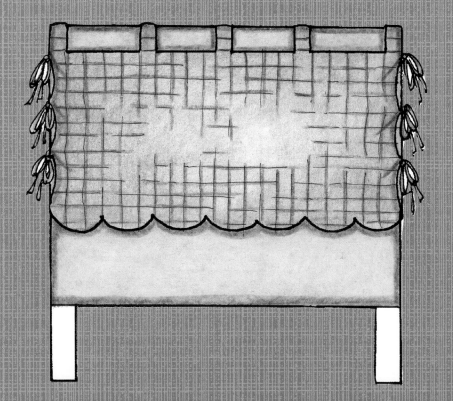

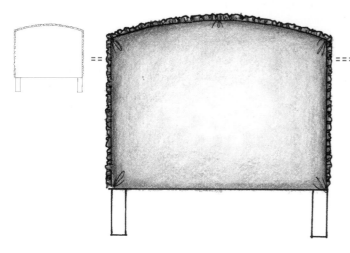

This simple cover is embellished with a short ruffle that follows the outline of the headboard. Headboard slipcovers should be fitted closely and secured in place to avoid shifting and twisting of the cover over time.

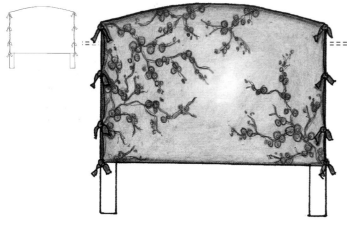

A pretty printed fabric is used for this slipcover that is open at the two sides of the headboard. Contrasting ties placed at even intervals down the open edge of the cover are knotted together, holding the cover in place. The solid fabric of the upholstered headboard shows through at the two sides of the cover.

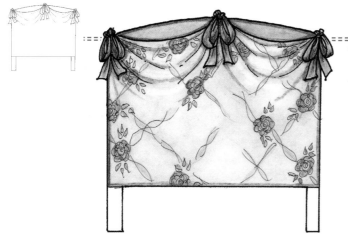

The top of this cover is designed to swag over the existing headboard, exposing a portion of the fabric underneath. The cover is anchored at the top with large bows. Each bow is firmly attached to the back of the headboard.

Contrasting bands of fabric run down the inside of this cover that is split into three sections at the face. The contrasting fabric is exposed at the openings of the three panels and matching bows tie the panels together.

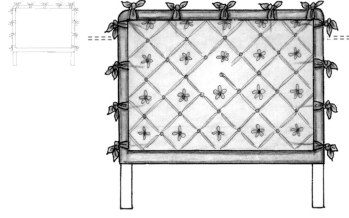

This partial cover consists of two flat panels, one for the front and one for the back of the headboard. Fabric ties are placed evenly around the edge of the two panels and tied together to hold the panels in place. This style of cover can be used on an upholstered or hard surface headboard.

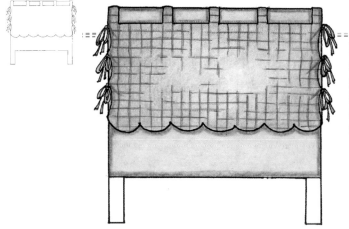

In this design a front and back panel with scalloped hems are joined together at the top by a series of fabric tabs. The panels are folded over the headboard and tied into place by long ties knotted into bows at each side. The fabric of the headboard shows through, creating a contrasting background.

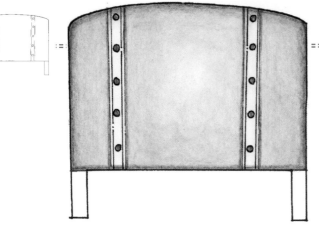

A pair of false plackets, with buttons resembling the front of a man's shirt, are the focal point of this tailored cover. When using buttons on an area that will be in contact with the body, use flat or slightly rounded buttons that won't cause discomfort. Be sure they are sewn securely in place with heavy-duty thread to avoid having them come loose or tear off, damaging the fabric of the cover.

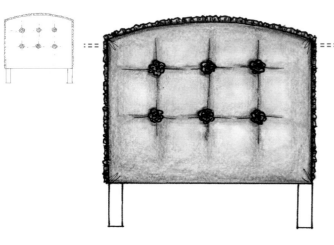

The illusion of an upholstered headboard with tufting can be achieved by applying a layer of batting to the face of the slipcover. Rosettes are attached in a typical tufting pattern, creating the look. A small ruffle running around the edge of the cover accents the rosettes.

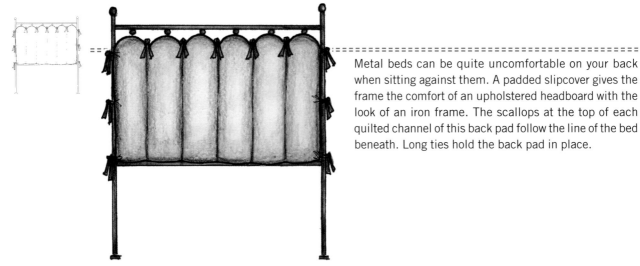

Metal beds can be quite uncomfortable on your back when sitting against them. A padded slipcover gives the frame the comfort of an upholstered headboard with the look of an iron frame. The scallops at the top of each quilted channel of this back pad follow the line of the bed beneath. Long ties hold the back pad in place.

On many iron beds, it is only necessary to pad the lower portion of the headboard for comfort, leaving the top half exposed. This pad has loops that thread around the back slats of the headboard and attach to the back pad with hook-and-loop tape. Decorative ties hold the sides of the pad in place. The pad is tufted with three buttons across the center.

Back pads can be a great addition to a wood headboard. This pad has an outside channel of padding that rims the center pad. Small ruffles trim the inner and outer edges. Fabric loops fitted with hook-and-loop tape attach the back pad to the back surface of the headboard. Ties secure the pad to the headboard at each side.

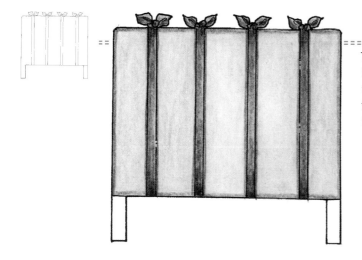

The long ribbons and ties that embellish this fitted headboard cover are just for show. The cover is constructed with two hidden zippers at each side to provide a snug fit and to allow the cover to be installed easily over the headboard.

Grommets and laces appear to be holding this headboard cover together but they are just for decoration. The cover has a hidden opening at the back for easy application and removal of the cover.

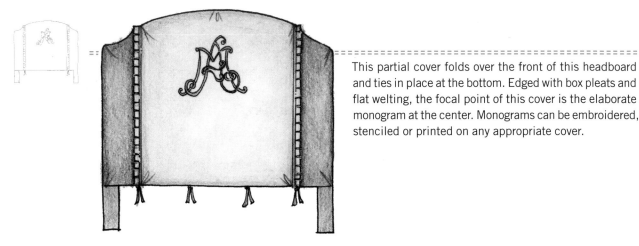

This partial cover folds over the front of this headboard and ties in place at the bottom. Edged with box pleats and flat welting, the focal point of this cover is the elaborate monogram at the center. Monograms can be embroidered, stenciled or printed on any appropriate cover.

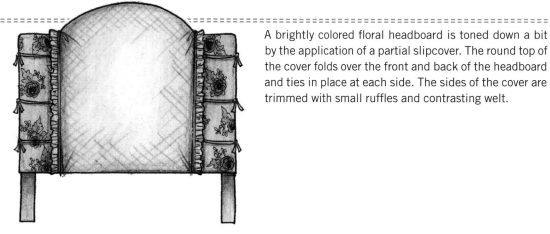

A brightly colored floral headboard is toned down a bit by the application of a partial slipcover. The round top of the cover folds over the front and back of the headboard and ties in place at each side. The sides of the cover are trimmed with small ruffles and contrasting welt.

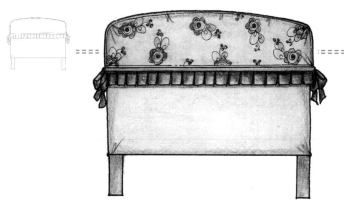

Sometimes called a dust cover, this style of slipcover is applied only to the top of the headboard. Trimmed in contrasting welt and a bold row of box pleats, this is a quick fix for any headboard that might have a bit of wear and tear at the top.

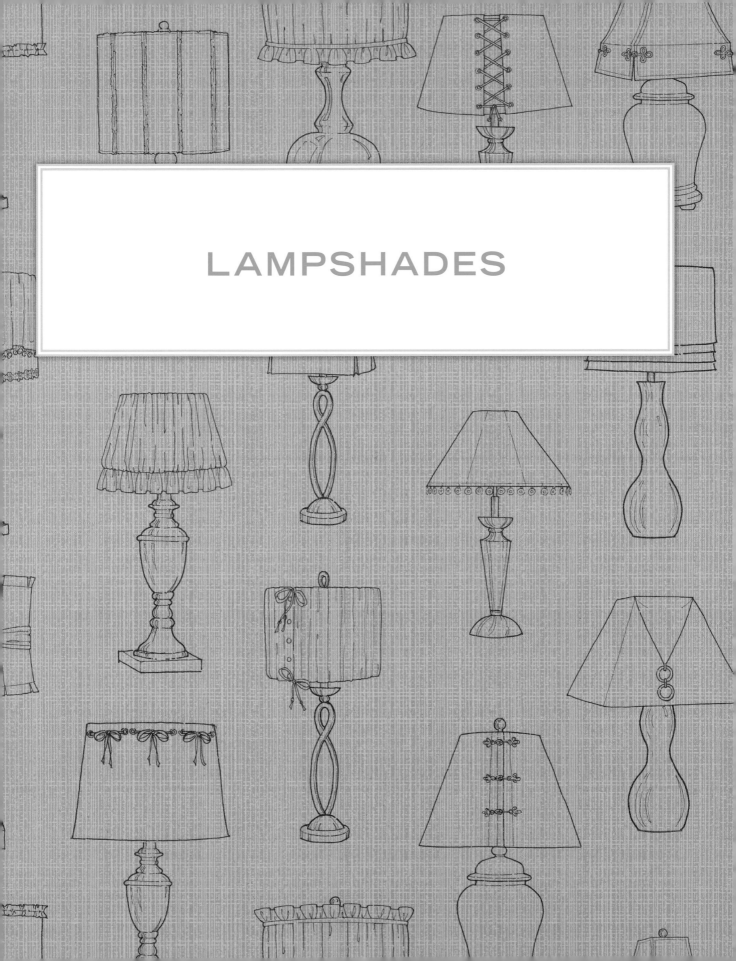

LAMPSHADES

Lampshade covers can instantly transform your light fixtures and add new color and detail to your room. They are fairly easy to construct and they can be changed often.

Safety is a concern when designing lampshade covers.

Be sure that the fabric is placed well clear of the lightbulb and the switch of the lamp.

Do not cover the top opening of the shade. This area not only lets light escape but also vents heat that builds off the lightbulb.

Make sure to use the recommended wattage for the bulbs in the fixture to prevent overheating and possible fire hazard.

TAILORED LAMPSHADE COVERS

For shade slipcovers that you want to fit snugly, it is best to use traditional closures at the back of the shade. This will allow you to achieve a tailored look that will keep your covers securely in place.

Hook-and-Loop Tape

Hook-and-Eye Tape

Ties

Buttonhole and Buttons

LOOSE-FITTING LAMPSHADE COVERS

Loose-fitting shades can be constructed as one piece and pulled over the lampshade. This eliminates the need for closers at the back of the shade and allows you to achieve a cleaner look.

It is important to note that this does not work for all types and shapes of lampshades.

The shade must be smaller in diameter or overall measurement at the top than at the bottom to prevent the slip from falling off. Shades that are only slightly smaller at the top may require an anchor tie that connects the slip to the shade to prevent drooping.

This type of cover will usually have a more casual and slouchy appearance than a tightly tailored one. It is best to use fabric that has a bit of flexibility and drape to it so you have some wriggle room when installing the cover.

Four sharp pleats are placed around the perimeter of this cover and topped with contrasting fabric-covered buttons.

A series of small tucks are sewn into sections of this cover, creating rows of texture in the fabric. A wide ribbon is tied around the shade and knotted into a bow at the front.

This cover is cut on the radius to create a flouncy ruffle with no bulk at the top. Decorative braid is used to trim the top edge of the cover and create a double bow with key tassels hanging down the face.

Quilted leaves and a handmade rosette are used to trim this cover. The edge is finished with a knife-pleated ruffle.

The fabric panels that make up this lampshade cover are sewn together with the seams facing front. The edges are left raw and cut with a zigzag edge. A ribbon band with a rosette finishes off the design.

This cover is fitted closely to the shade and embellished with a velvet sash. A carved wooden medallion is set in the center of the sash.

When applying a ribbon or sash to your lamp cover, be sure to tack it in place in a few spots to keep it from sagging or pulling down the rest of the cover.

Double rows of ruffles bind the edges of this feminine lampshade cover.

This cover has a wide band of contrasting fabric running around the perimeter of the shade just above the bottom hem. Large rosettes are placed on top of the band, creating a floral border.

Matching ruffles in two different sizes trim the top and bottom edges of this tailored cover.

The ruffles on this cover are placed vertically down the face rather than in the more common horizontal position, creating a striped effect around the shade cover.

This shirred cover has a simple elastic band sewn into the heading that is topped with a fabric band with a double bow at the front.

This flat, ruffle-edged cover requires a securing mechanism such as an elastic band or cross ties at the top of the shade to hold it in place.

The top of this double-layered cover is a shirred skirt that is attached to a flat under layer. The top of the cover is secured in place over the shade with an elastic banding.

This tightly fitted cover has wide pleated ruffles at the top and bottom of the shade. The fabric tie is attached to the cover and ties in a knot at the front.

This rustic shade cover is sewn together with the raw edges of the fabric exposed and sewn into rows around the perimeter of the shade. The top and bottom of the shade are left raw as well.

Elastic is fitted into casings at the top of this cover, and a few inches above the bottom volume created by the elastic allows the fabric to have a balloon effect above the bottom casing and ruffle.

Small grommets are placed in pairs at the top of this shade cover. Ribbons are threaded through them and tied in a series of bows, creating a unique border.

Two rows of knife pleats run around the bottom of this simple shade cover a few inches apart from one another.

Bands of fabric at the top and the bottom of this shade cover hold the shirred fabric of the center panel and the ruffles in place.

This square shade is covered with four panels of fabric, pleated at the corners and tied in place at the top and center of the panels.

Casings at the top and bottom of this cover are threaded with elastic to shirr the fabric of the cover at both edges. The closure of this cover is decorative with contrasting buttons and ties in plain view.

The lampshade of this lamp is exposed where the two opening edges of the cover are fitted with grommets and laced together.

Any lampshade cover can be dressed up with a bit of decorative trim or fringe. This cover is embellished with a beaded trim at the hem.

Decorative frog closures are a great way to add detail to a lamp cover. In this design, they are used to close the opening of the cover and provide decorative interest at the same time.

In this design, decorative frogs are used at pairs on the corners of the shade skirt. The panels of the cover are trimmed in contrasting banding to emphasize the interesting shape of the lampshade.

This modern cover is designed with multiple layers of fabric, each one longer than the last, stacking up at the bottom hem.

RESOURCES

These schools and associations provide expert training, support and certification for professional slipcover artisans. Most include a directory of qualified members in your area on their websites.

Custom Home Furnishings School
13900 South Lakes Drive, Suite F
Charlotte, NC 28273
800-222-1415
704-333-4636
704-333-4639
info@CHFschool.com
www.draperyschool.com

Custom Home Sewing Institute
1318 Sue Barnett Drive
Houston, TX 77018
713.697.4110
info@csisews.com

Slipcover America, Inc.
914 Repetto Drive
St. Louis, M) 63122
800-267-4958
karen@slipcoveramerica.com
www.slipcoveramerica.net

Slipcover Network
Karen Erickson
2801 Bickford Avenue, Suite 103, PMB 128
Snohomish, WA 98290
slipcovernetwrok@gmail.com
www.slipcovernetwork

Workroom Association of America
www.waoamembersite.com
802 North Robinson Drive
Waco, TX 76706
254-662-4021
info@workroomassociation.com

WCAA
Window Coverings Association of America
2646 Highway 109, Suite 205
Grover, MO 63040
888-298-9222
636-273-4439
www.wcaa.org

WFCP
Window Fashions Certification Program
Grace McNamara, Inc.
4215 White Bear Parkway, Suite 100
St. Paul, MN 55110
(651) 293-1544
(651) 653-4308
www.wfcppro.com

ACKNOWLEDGMENTS

I would like to extend a special thanks to Christy Statz, Linda Meeks, Cozy Cottage Slipcovers, Emily Petit, Kippi O'Hern, Teresa Bennet, Deb Fowler, Barbara Roth, Jackie, and my dear friend Beth Hodges for their help.